I0047842

THE PHILIPPINES COUNTRY KNOWLEDGE STRATEGY AND PLAN, 2012–2017

A KNOWLEDGE COMPENDIUM

JUNE 2021

ADB

ASIAN DEVELOPMENT BANK

Creative Commons Attribution 3.0 IGO license (CC BY 3.0 IGO)

© 2021 Asian Development Bank
6 ADB Avenue, Mandaluyong City, 1550 Metro Manila, Philippines
Tel +63 2 8632 4444; Fax +63 2 8636 2444
www.adb.org

Some rights reserved. Published in 2021.

ISBN 978-92-9262-901-4 (print); 978-92-9262-902-1 (electronic); 978-92-9262-903-8 (ebook)
Publication Stock No. TCS210198-2
DOI http://dx.doi.org/10.22617/TCS210198-2

The views expressed in this publication are those of the authors and do not necessarily reflect the views and policies of the Asian Development Bank (ADB) or its Board of Governors or the governments they represent.

ADB does not guarantee the accuracy of the data included in this publication and accepts no responsibility for any consequence of their use. The mention of specific companies or products of manufacturers does not imply that they are endorsed or recommended by ADB in preference to others of a similar nature that are not mentioned.

By making any designation of or reference to a particular territory or geographic area, or by using the term "country" in this document, ADB does not intend to make any judgments as to the legal or other status of any territory or area.

This work is available under the Creative Commons Attribution 3.0 IGO license (CC BY 3.0 IGO) https://creativecommons.org/licenses/by/3.0/igo/. By using the content of this publication, you agree to be bound by the terms of this license. For attribution, translations, adaptations, and permissions, please read the provisions and terms of use at https://www.adb.org/terms-use#openaccess.

This CC license does not apply to non-ADB copyright materials in this publication. If the material is attributed to another source, please contact the copyright owner or publisher of that source for permission to reproduce it. ADB cannot be held liable for any claims that arise as a result of your use of the material.

Please contact pubsmarketing@adb.org if you have questions or comments with respect to content, or if you wish to obtain copyright permission for your intended use that does not fall within these terms, or for permission to use the ADB logo.

Corrigenda to ADB publications may be found at http://www.adb.org/publications/corrigenda.

Notes:
In this publication, "$" refers to United States dollars.

Cover design by Edith Creus.

Contents

Figures

Figures

Abbreviations

ADB	Asian Development Bank
AEC	ASEAN Economic Community
ASEAN	Association of Southeast Asian Nations
BIMP-EAGA	Brunei Darussalam–Indonesia–Malaysia–Philippines East ASEAN Growth Area
CCT	conditional cash transfer
CDD	community-driven development
CPS	country partnership strategy
CKP	Country Knowledge Program
CTI	Coral Triangle Initiative
DMC	developing member country
DOLE	Department of Labor and Employment
DSWD	Department of Social Welfare and Development
GEF	Global Environment Facility
KALAHI-CIDSS	*Kapit-Bisig Laban sa Kahirapan* Comprehensive and Integrated Delivery of Social Services
KPS	knowledge product and service
LGU	local government unit
MSMEs	micro, small, and medium-sized enterprises
NPOA	national plan of action
PPP	public–private partnership
NEDA	National Economic and Development Authority
TA	technical assistance

1 Knowledge Products and Services in the Philippines

Introduction

Knowledge is critical in addressing the complex challenges of development and poverty reduction faced by the Philippines today. In its new, long-term strategy leading to 2030, *Strategy 2030* (ADB 2018a), the Asian Development Bank (ADB) recognizes its value as a knowledge provider and acknowledges that its continued relevance increasingly depends on its role as a knowledge institution. Strategy 2030 notes that "even when developing member countries (DMCs) can tap other sources of financing, clients often turn to ADB for...the sharing of knowledge, skills, and expertise accumulated over more than 50 years of ADB working together with DMCs." The development of knowledge solutions in ADB is guided and supported by the Knowledge Management Directions and Action Plan, 2013–2015 (ADB 2013p), which has four main goals: (i) prioritizing and implementing knowledge solutions; (ii) enriching the quality of ADB and DMC knowledge capabilities for development effectiveness; (iii) advancing ADB's knowledge assets, information systems, and communications; and (iv) empowering and resourcing high-quality knowledge solutions.

The Finance++ Approach in the action plan envisages the combination of attractive financing, strategic partnerships, and high-quality knowledge as a way to maximize and accelerate development effectiveness. The development of knowledge solutions under this approach is demand driven and client oriented, ensured by applying the ADB operations cycle to organize knowledge needs identification and generation, capture, and dissemination of knowledge products and services (Figure 1).

Figure 1: Knowledge from the Operations Cycle

Knowledge from the Operations Cycle

- Economic, thematic, and sector analyses and work
- Country Programming
- Policy, project-specific analyses, and advice during preparation
- Project Preparation
- Capacity development, training, advisory and analytical support, and monitoring and evaluation
- Project Implementation
- Operations Evaluation
- Evaluation at completion, lessons, and better practice identified

Philippines Development Plan

Source: Asian Development Bank. 2012. *Philippines Country Operations Business Plan, 2013–2015*. Manila.

The Philippines Country Knowledge Strategy and Plan, 2012–2017

The Philippines Country Knowledge Strategy and Plan, 2012–2017 was the first strategy to be completed under ADB's Finance ++ Approach. The plan was designed to be integral to the Philippines Country Partnership Strategy (CPS), 2011–2016[1] (ADB 2011a) and support its overarching objective to help the Philippines achieve high, inclusive, and sustainable growth. The strategy aligns with the principle that all knowledge content arising from the CPS lending and non-lending program is based on country needs and demand, which in turn arise from country, sector, and thematic analyses, strategies and road maps, and related government dialogue. The strategy thus acknowledges that knowledge support is largely embedded in the ADB advisory and analytical work, loans, and technical assistance delivered through operations. The strategy encompasses economic, sector, and thematic knowledge work across the main strategic directions of ADB support (Figure 2).

Figure 2: Main Themes of the Philippines Country Knowledge Strategy

ADB Support to the Philippines

- Sustainable and Climate-Resilient Infrastructure
- Governance and Inclusive Finance
- Employment and Education
- Regional Cooperation and Integration

Implementation of Country Partnership Strategy, 2011–2016

Public Infrastructure and Public–Private Partnerships
- Sustainable Transport
- Connectivity and Logistics

Utilities and Services
- Water Security
- Solid Waste Management
- Disaster Risk Management

- Nonbank and Capital Market Reforms
- Inclusive Finance
- Public Sector Management
- Local Government Finance

- Rural Enterprise and Employment
- Youth Employment
- K to 12 and Education Quality
- Social Protection: Conditional Cash Transfer

ASEAN Integration Program
Brunei Darussalam–Indonesia–Malaysia–Philippines East ASEAN Growth Area

Knowledge Products and Services

ASEAN = Association of Southeast Asian Nations.
Source: ADB Philippines Country Office.

From 2012 to 2017, the output of ADB knowledge products and services that supported CPS implementation has been substantial. In preparing this report, more than 200 knowledge products and services were identified as either directly related to Philippine operations or having substantial contents relevant to Philippine development (Appendix). The list in the appendix is not exhaustive; many knowledge products and services employed during

---

[1]   The 2011–2016 CPS was extended to 2017.

the implementation of technical assistance (TA) projects remain unpublished and/or are documented only in individual project archives and reports. Moreover, the list in the appendix is not a comprehensive record, as it only presents examples of the coverage and nature of knowledge products and services (KPS) used during the said time period.

It must be acknowledged that the quantity of KPS delivered cannot adequately measure their ultimate value and effectiveness in ADB operations in the Philippines, yet some general trends can be drawn from the list reviewed. The spread of KPS across sectors strongly reflects the developing strategic directions during the period 2012–2017. Good governance and inclusive finance represented 25% of total KPS; education, employment, and social protection (19%); sustainable and climate-resilient infrastructure (16%); and regional cooperation and integration comprised (16%)—altogether, these sectors accounted for nearly 80% of the listed KPS.

Figure 3: Selected Knowledge Products and Services by Sector, Actual Count and Share, 2012–2017

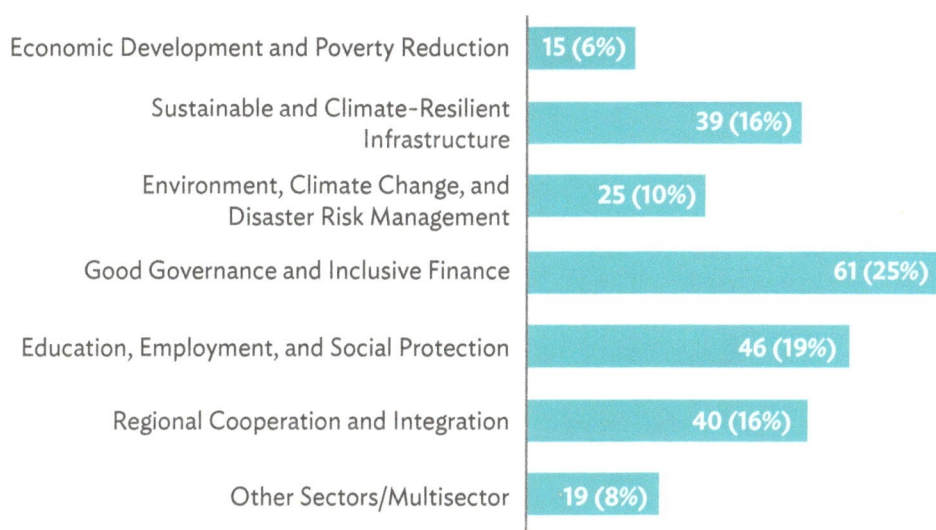

Sector	Count (Share)
Economic Development and Poverty Reduction	15 (6%)
Sustainable and Climate-Resilient Infrastructure	39 (16%)
Environment, Climate Change, and Disaster Risk Management	25 (10%)
Good Governance and Inclusive Finance	61 (25%)
Education, Employment, and Social Protection	46 (19%)
Regional Cooperation and Integration	40 (16%)
Other Sectors/Multisector	19 (8%)

Source: ADB Philippines Country Office.

Objectives and Structure of the Report

At the first ADB Knowledge Forum held in 2018, ADB Vice-President for Knowledge Management and Sustainable Development Bambang Susantono pointed out in his opening remarks that "Knowledge, whether explicit or tacit, is of not much worth unless it is put into practice. It needs to be deployed, demonstrated, and disseminated to ensure its true value." Thus, this report organizes and makes more accessible all explicit and tacit knowledge employed by ADB's operations in the Philippines during 2012–2017. It includes knowledge gleaned from deep collaboration with the Government of the Philippines and other development partners. This report aims to contribute to greater development effectiveness by informing future operations and country planning with fit-for-purpose lessons and good practices from past experiences, within specific sectors and themes. It provides a qualitative insight into how knowledge solutions were identified, developed, and utilized, and how knowledge contributed to the evolving partnership with the Philippines during 2012–2017.

This report covers the four areas of operations that reflect the strategic directions of ADB support in the Philippines. It also covers economy-wide and poverty reduction issues, while integrating cross-cutting issues such as gender, private sector development, and capacity development. Each section highlights significant knowledge solutions and their utilization. It also includes summaries of KPS from the list in the Appendix to demonstrate particularly valuable contributions to ADB operations and/or good knowledge practice. The sections are as follows:

(i)   economic development and poverty reduction;

(ii)   sustainable and climate-resilient infrastructure;

(iii)   environment, climate change, and disaster risk management;

(iv)   good governance and inclusive finance;

(v)   education, employment, and social protection; and

(vi)   regional cooperation and integration.

Finally, this report looks ahead to consider how knowledge requirements are evolving in the Philippines, including the anticipated knowledge needs for the next CPS and for the current Philippines Country Partnership Strategy, 2018–2023 (ADB 2018b); and how ADB is responding to these demands.

2 Progress and Achievements, 2012–2017

Economic Development and Poverty Reduction

The Philippine economy has grown steadily in the last decade with gross domestic product (GDP) growth averaging 6.4% annually from 2010 to 2019, one of the fastest-growing economies in Southeast Asia. Strong growth, however, has yet to deliver a sustained increase in quality employment to further reduce poverty in the country. The government has intensified efforts to sustain strong growth and to ensure that the benefits of growth are shared more across the population. The ADB 2011–2016 CPS directly supported this goal, with access to knowledge as a critical aspect of the partnership, addressing the complex challenge of inclusive growth through (i) the provision of analysis and advisory work, (ii) policy dialogue, (iii) sector and thematic studies, and (iv) various economic forums. The CPS, 2018–2023 for the Philippines remains committed to ensuring that knowledge and innovation are an integral part of its lending and technical support operations.

Two milestone knowledge products directly supported the preparation and implementation of the 2011–2016 CPS. These are (i) *Taking the Right Road to Inclusive Growth: Industrial Upgrading and Diversification in the Philippines* (ADB 2012c), and (ii) *Private Sector Development: Challenges and Possible Ways to Go* (ADB 2011b). The first study—on economic transformation—was a critical input to the development of the CPS and was also widely disseminated in various forums conducted for the academia, industry, and local government units in the Philippines. The second sector study provided both macroeconomic and microeconomic perspectives on sector development by highlighting the country's key constraints and reviewing the options for ADB support during CPS implementation. Further studies done on private sector development reviewed the role and potential of the service sector, particularly small and medium-sized enterprises, as a focus for inclusive growth (ADB 2012d, 2013a, and 2013b).

In response to positive political developments in Mindanao during the 2011–2016 CPS implementation, ADB is increasing its engagement and expanding its portfolio as reflected in the Country Operations Business Plan, 2019–2021 (ADB 2018c). A knowledge-focused TA strengthened Mindanao institutions in support of public sector investments, including the preparation of a capacity development program approach for the Mindanao Development Authority, Bangsamoro Development Agency, and Autonomous Region in Muslim Mindanao (ADB 2015a). The TA also undertook a critical study on Mindanao growth corridors development to bolster infrastructure and improve transport and logistics support to tourism, industry, and agriculture sectors.

ADB supported the National Economic and Development Authority (NEDA) in the preparation of a landmark long-term vision of the country's development—*AmBisyon Natin 2040* (NEDA 2017). This sets out the goals and aspirations of the country based on in-depth socioeconomic studies and wide citizen consultation. ADB assisted in this exercise by preparing thematic studies and scenarios to help frame the long-term strategic development vision and to identify development paths and options for the Philippines over the coming years to sustain its inclusive growth and prepare for other long-term development challenges.

Summaries of Selected Knowledge Products

AmBisyon Natin 2040 (2017). AmBisyon Natin 2040 represents the collective long-term vision and aspirations of the Filipino people for themselves and the country in the coming years. This is expressed in the vision statement: "By 2040, Filipinos enjoy a strongly rooted, comfortable, and secure life." AmBisyon Natin 2040 is the result of a long-term visioning process that began in 2015. President Rodrigo Duterte signed an executive order on 11 October 2016 adopting the 25-year long-term vision for the country. All future Philippine development plans to be crafted and implemented until 2040 will be anchored on AmBisyon Natin 2040. This will ensure the sustainability and consistency of government strategies, policies, programs, and projects across political administrations.

Capacity Development for Growth and Poverty Reduction in Mindanao and Bangsamoro: A Medium- to Long-Term Approach (2017). This presentation was given at the ADB-Asian Development Bank Institute Forum on Governance and Institutions: Practical Lessons on Governance and Service Delivery for Subnational Governments. It discusses the potential of the country's second largest island, Mindanao, to contribute more to the development of the Philippines. Poor capacity, institutional weakness, and ineffective service delivery hinder the effective implementation of local development plans and investment programs in the different regions comprising Mindanao. Addressing this challenge will require improving coordination, strengthening institutional mechanisms, and promoting capacity development.

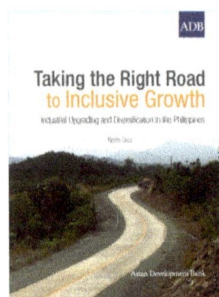

Taking the Right Road to Inclusive Growth: Industrial Upgrading and Diversification in the Philippines **(2012).** This study helps policy makers and other stakeholders understand the fundamental structural and policy challenges to long-term economic development in the Philippines. It also helps policy makers design and implement policies for structural change based on a long-term vision for inclusive growth. The study sets out to discover why the Philippines, despite its favorable economic conditions and strong service sector, has not achieved growth comparable to its neighbors and why the chronic problems of unemployment, poverty, and low investment continue to persist.

Sustainable and Climate-Resilient Infrastructure

Public–Private Partnerships

Like many of its neighbors in Southeast Asia, the Philippines is facing a major gap in infrastructure finance. The government considers public–private partnerships (PPPs) as critical in closing this gap. From 2012 to 2016, there was rapid progress in the enabling environment for PPPs and in project development. ADB has been a major partner in this work, particularly in supporting the establishment and building the capacity of the Public-Private Partnership (PPP) Center—a one-stop shop for promoting, coordinating, advising, and monitoring PPPs in the country. The development of the center was knowledge-driven, and ADB TA provided a comprehensive review of the PPP institutional setup (ADB 2011c). It also provided support in developing manuals and sector guidelines for local government units (LGUs) and national government agencies, and in preparing the series of policy briefs aimed to push for amendments to a PPP-relevant legislation. The project also devised and set up a knowledge management system for the PPP Center website, including an e-library that provides implementing agencies with up-to-date information on best practice.

Knowledge support for PPP development also focused on the education and health sectors. A major conference on PPPs in education in 2014 organized jointly by ADB, the PPP Center, the Department of Education, and the Department of Finance shared best practices in policy, technology, and finance in support of the Philippines' Kindergarten to Grade 12 (K to 12) basic education reform program (ADB 2014b). In the health sector, the Credit for Better Health Care Project sponsored a learning forum on best practices for health sector PPPs in the Philippines, discussing the main barriers to implementing and initiating a policy dialogue on the adoption of PPPs in the country (ADB 2009a). The TA also developed guidelines for PPP implementation across a number of health services (ADB 2013c and 2013d), and established a knowledge and resources hub for health PPPs in the Philippines.

Summaries of Selected Knowledge Products

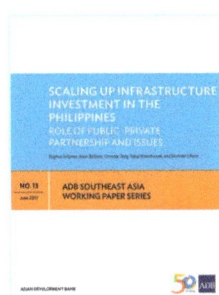

***Scaling Up Infrastructure Investment in the Philippines: Role of Public–Private Partnership and Issues* (2017).** This publication analyzes PPP arrangements in the Philippines and their critical role in improving infrastructure investment standards. The paper outlines issues in (i) the choice between public procurement (including overseas development assistance) and PPPs, (ii) the implementation and monitoring of PPP projects, and (iii) fiscal risks in general and how they apply to the Philippines. It also looks into the Philippine experience of embarking into the PPP modality—from various dimensions—and points out key challenges that need to be overcome. This publication recommends policies to help the government mobilize private sector expertise and resources to improve PPP project screening, approval, and implementation.

***Learning from International Experience: Innovative Public–Private Partnerships in the Education Sector* (Philippines, November 2014)**. This learning event was organized jointly by ADB, the PPP Center, the Department of Education, and the Department of Finance. It aimed to share best international practices in policy, technology, and finance to support the Philippines' K to 12 education reform agenda. This program extends basic education to include a prerequisite kindergarten and two additional years of senior high school. Participants included selected government officials, experts, professionals, and business leaders from the Philippine infrastructure and education sectors. The learning event showcased successful case studies and best international practices, highlighted key lessons, and introduced innovative approaches to infrastructure PPP in education. Final discussions centered on the barriers to implementing PPPs and the opportunities that could advance the Philippine agenda for reform.

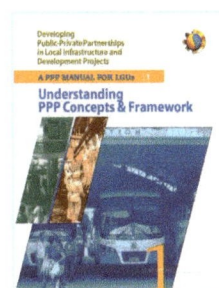

***Developing Public–Private Partnerships in Local Infrastructure and Development Projects: A PPP Manual for Local Government Units* (2012)**. Three volumes of manuals were prepared by NEDA, the Department of Interior and Local Government, and the Development Academy of the Philippines with the support of ADB and the World Bank. These manuals provide a comprehensive framework and detailed guidance for LGUs that develop and implement PPP infrastructure projects according to the principles of good governance. The manuals have assisted the PPP Center and LGUs in developing LGU PPP projects. The first LGU-initiated project was approved in early 2015.

Sustainable Transport

Traffic congestion, longer travel times and high costs, and deteriorating local air quality have a big impact on the economy and human health in the rapidly growing cities of the Philippines. City governments are increasingly aware that a modernized, efficient, and affordable public transport system is part of the solution. In Davao City, ADB worked with the local government to create an enabling environment for improved and sustainable urban transport (ADB 2012e). Such an approach meant moving beyond business as usual not just for government regulators, but for all stakeholders, such as operators, drivers, and passengers. Knowledge solutions helped in (i) raising the awareness and understanding of stakeholders on the proposed reforms, (ii) convincing them of the value of the approach, and (iii) building a consensus and momentum for change. In this process, the important milestones included reviews of existing transport systems, plans, and service procurement; and the crucial development of a comprehensive transport strategy (ADB 2013f). Under the TA, conducting a series of knowledge events facilitated greater understanding, wider consultation, and consensus building. These included holding forums with key stakeholder groups, pursuing a capacity development program for city technical officers, and launching workshops on various aspects of sustainable transport (ADB 2013f). These activities culminated in the Davao Transport Summit in 2013 where participants committed to a shared vision and continuing support to the reform program.

Summaries of Selected Knowledge Products

The Impact of Improved Transport Connectivity on Income, Education, and Health: The Case of the Roll-On, Roll-Off System in the Philippines **(2017)**. This report analyzes the impacts of providing an efficient and affordable transport system based on the Philippine experience. It also discusses the additional effects beyond economic growth when physical linkages among local economies within a country are strengthened. In 2003, the roll-on/roll-off (Ro-Ro) policy was implemented in the Philippines to provide an integrated mode of interisland transfer. Agricultural households largely benefited from the Ro-Ro port operation. There was also higher school attendance in municipalities near Ro-Ro ports. The study also reveals lower household consumption of alcoholic beverages and tobacco in areas near Ro-Ro ports. The report highlights the crucial role of the transport system in a country's socioeconomic development.

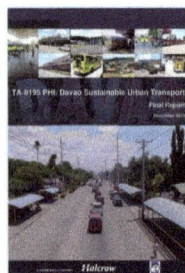

Davao Sustainable Transport Project: Final Report **(2015)**. This report summarizes the project and provides the project context—a review of Davao City's urban and transport plans and the existing public transport. It also presents a comprehensive public transport strategy for the city developed under the TA. The strategy covers transport operations; support infrastructure and facilities; contracting, franchising, and financial management arrangements; institutional and organizational arrangements; and social impacts and capacity development needs.

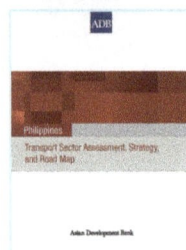

Philippines: Transport Sector Assessment, Strategy, and Road Map **(2012)**. This document tackles development issues, needs, and strategic assistance priorities of the Government of the Philippines and ADB, with a focus on roads and intermodal integration, governance and institutional capacity, urban transport, and private sector infrastructure development. It highlights sector performance, priority development constraints, the government's strategy and plans, other development partner support, lessons learned from past ADB support, and possible future ADB assistance, including knowledge support and investments. The report provides the basis for further dialogue on how ADB and the government can work together in managing the challenges of transport sector development in the Philippines in the coming years.

Davao City Transport Summit (Philippines, November 2013). The Davao City Transport Summit, facilitated by the Davao Sustainable Transport Project (page 8), was the culmination of an intensive stakeholder consultation on the city's changing transport needs and options for future development. Participants reviewed the progress in developing the transport strategy and formed a mechanism for regular engagement among the city's major transport stakeholders. The event was attended by representatives of the city government, national government agencies related to transport, transport user groups, transport providers, ADB staff, consultants, and the media. Following this summit, transport management was brought under a single local agency.

Water Supply

Rapid urbanization in the Philippines continues to stretch the capacity of urban infrastructure services and facilities. Many water providers struggle to effectively supply safe water and sustainable sanitation services. Yet, there have been some high-profile successes in Manila and elsewhere that are significantly contributing to country and regional knowledge sharing on water and sanitation best practice—through ADB technical assistance. The ADB Water Operators' Partnerships Program (ADB 2011d) facilitated knowledge sharing on nonrevenue water between Maynilad Water Services, Inc., a private sector operator in Manila, and a similar entity planning new investments in Bangladesh. The project is supporting similar knowledge partnerships between the Manila Water Company, Inc. and utility operators in Cambodia, Palawan, and Phnom Penh. The project also produced a flagship publication, *Tap Secrets* (ADB and Manila Water Company 2014), which discussed lessons learned from the Manila Water Company's transformation into a commercially viable and effective utility service. The TA, Promoting Innovations in Wastewater Management in Asia and the Pacific (ADB 2012f), disseminated lessons on wastewater management from successful Philippine initiatives (ADB 2014c), and convened a capacity-building workshop for water districts in the Philippines, which prepared them for their participation in the Water District Development Sector Project supported by ADB.

Summaries of Selected Knowledge Products

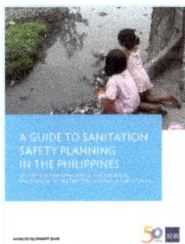

A Guide to Sanitation Safety Planning in the Philippines **(2016)**. This guide describes a six-step process in sanitation safety planning in the Philippines, based on the pilot project experiences of two water service providers—the Baliwag Water District and the Maynilad Water Services, Inc. This document encourages other utilities that operate sanitation facilities in the Philippines to do sanitation safety planning and to develop their own incremental improvement plans.

Water Operators' Partnerships Case Study: Twinning Khulna WASA and Maynilad **(2014).** This case study—drawn from an ADB regional TA program—describes the twinning of an experienced water utility, the privately owned Maynilad Water Services, Inc. (Maynilad), as mentor to the Khulna Water and Sewerage Authority (Kulna WASA), which operates in Bangladesh's third largest city. A major expansion of the city's water supply infrastructure—supported by ADB and the Government of Japan—will allow Khulna WASA to increase its customer base from 18,000 to 1.5 million. Such a rapid expansion presents many challenges, particularly in managing water loss and moving from unmetered to metered water distribution. Through a number of visits by management and engineers from each organization, Maynilad demonstrated to Khulna WASA the effective techniques for reducing water loss and how to roll out a water metering program. One strategy shared by Maynilad was the establishment of district metered areas to detect, measure, and manage water losses—which was successfully established in Khulna. Maynilad also supported Khulna WASA in the sensitive but necessary task of introducing customers to water metering.

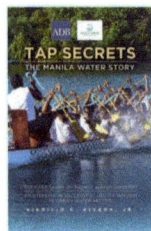

***Tap Secrets: The Manila Water Story* (2014).** This publication describes how the Manila Water Company, Inc. was transformed from an ailing public water utility into a successful private service organization. It provides lessons from this experience and shares good practices. The book continues to be used by diverse groups, such as executives of infrastructure and utility companies in the Philippines and abroad, human resource and organization experts, journalists, academicians, and researchers whose works focus on PPPs in water utilities.

Environment, Climate Change, and Disaster Risk Management

Disaster Risk Management and Response

The Philippines is prone to natural hazards, with around 20 typhoons hitting the country every year, which inflict loss of life and cause significant damage to the economy. In November 2013, the country was struck by one of the strongest typhoons ever to make landfall. Typhoon Haiyan (known locally as Yolanda) affected more than 12 million people, causing more than 6,000 deaths and devastating economies in the Visayas and northern Palawan regions. The response of ADB was immediate and substantial. It provided more than $900 million in loans and grants for the affected areas. Fast assimilation, analysis, and dissemination of knowledge are critical in disaster situations and have been central to ADB's response. This included support for the preparation of the government's rapid needs assessment (NEDA 2013) and a results framework for guiding and monitoring the typhoon recovery and rehabilitation program (NEDA 2014). A series of updates, articles, videos, and infographics on the ADB website kept stakeholders informed on the progress of ADB assistance and highlighted some of the stories of survivors. Lessons learned were gathered and disseminated; a report on experiences from post-Haiyan/Yolanda recovery planning and implementation was prepared (ADB 2015b), together with briefs on lessons from the reconstruction process and methodology and linking such recovery to development. A timely regional knowledge forum on post-disaster recovery held by ADB in October 2015 and November 2016 provided valuable opportunities for exchanging and documenting lessons from Haiyan/Yolanda and other recent disasters in Indonesia, Thailand, and the United States (ADB 2015c).

Summaries of Selected Knowledge Products

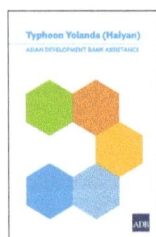

***Typhoon Yolanda (Haiyan): Asian Development Bank Assistance* (2014)**. ADB helped restore, repair, and rebuild critical infrastructure in typhoon Yolanda (Haiyan)-affected areas in the Philippines. It also provided conditional cash transfer programs and livelihood support for affected areas. This brochure provides an overview of ADB's assistance to areas hit by the typhoon and includes a detailed map of ADB-supported project activities for the repair and rehabilitation of community infrastructure in the Eastern Visayan region.

***Lessons from Community-Led Actions for Strengthening Disaster Resilience: A Case from the Philippines* (2017)**. This brief was produced under an ADB project—Support to Community-Based Disaster Risk Management in Southeast Asia (ADB 2013m). One of the initiatives featured demonstrated the leadership of community-based women's groups in integrating disaster-resilience priorities into development programs, with the help of LGUs. It also positioned community-based women's groups as knowledgeable partners—through networking and peer learning processes that rapidly transferred their practical knowledge.

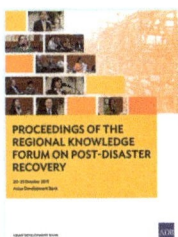

Proceedings of the Regional Knowledge Forum on Post-Disaster Recovery (2015).
This forum, organized by ADB in Manila in October 2015, became a venue for sharing common challenges and possible solutions on planning and managing recovery programs based on lessons and good practices. A number of key insights emerged from the discussions. First, post- disaster coordination processes should be built on existing country-led systems; should match the scale of the disaster; and include horizontal aspects (across sectors and jurisdictions) and vertical aspects (local, national, and international). Second, needs change as relief, recovery, and reconstruction move forward. Planning must be flexible enough to meet these evolving needs. Third, ensuring that the voice and aspirations of the communities are heard and acted upon promotes ownership of the process—contributing to its success. Fourth and final, successful recovery depends on strengthening the capacity of local governments and building a cadre of local experts. The forum was especially useful to participants from the Philippines who were then implementing a post-typhoon Haiyan/Yolanda recovery and reconstruction program.

Shared Lessons on Post-Disaster Recovery (2015). The Regional Knowledge Forum on Post-Disaster Recovery provided participants with a venue to exchange lessons from post-disaster recovery programs with national and local government officials from the Philippines. This brief summarizes the main themes and lessons discussed at the forum. These include (i) horizontal and vertical coordination, (ii) iterative planning, (iii) flexibility in implementation, (iv) speedy delivery, (v) maintenance of a culture of urgency, (vi) community and private sector engagement, (vii) strengthening of local capacity, (viii) active and constant communication, and (ix) managing of expectations.

Reconstruction Assistance on Yolanda: Implementation for Results (2014).
This document is the second of two planning documents prepared by NEDA to meet immediate post-disaster needs in areas affected by typhoon Haiyan/Yolanda. It presents an overall results framework for monitoring progress consistent with the country's Philippine Development Plan. It also highlights key policy and program initiatives that are being implemented or considered, covering livelihoods and business development, housing and resettlement, social services, and infrastructure.

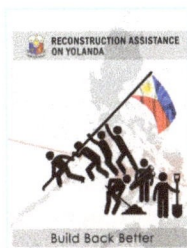

Reconstruction Assistance on Yolanda: Build Back Better (2013). This is the Philippine government's strategic plan to guide the recovery and rebuilding of the economy, lives, and livelihoods in the affected areas. It was published by NEDA on 13 December 2013, just over a month after typhoon Haiyan/Yolanda ravaged central Philippines. It was designed to guide rapid action in addressing critical and immediate needs, and to help develop and implement a full set of recovery and reconstruction interventions over the medium term.

Environment and Climate Change

Sustainable management of watersheds has become a critical issue in the Philippines. Ecological services are under threat as population pressure leads to deforestation and soil erosion, reducing the productivity of marginal upland farms and increasing the vulnerability of poor rural communities to natural calamities. In Mindanao, an ADB TA (ADB 2010a) delivered a wide range of knowledge solutions that enhanced the skills and expertise of the Department of Environment and Natural Resources, local government units (LGUs), and indigenous communities in sustainably managing watersheds and rural infrastructure. Experiences under this successful TA were documented in a compendium of knowledge products (ADB 2014d), which continued to support the original pilot LGUs. It also facilitated the rapid and effective roll out of watershed management activities on a larger scale under the Integrated Natural Resources and Environmental Management Project (ADB 2012g).

Climate change risk assessments at the watershed level have also become an essential knowledge product for guiding government investment planning, especially in a country like the Philippines, which is particularly vulnerable to the impacts of climate change. The preparation of a climate change atlas (ADB 2013g) for the Integrated Natural Resources and Environmental Management Project provided vulnerability assessments—to guide both community and LGU investments in sustainable watershed management.

Summaries of Selected Knowledge Products

Philippines: Integrated Natural Resources and Environmental Management Project Documents (ongoing). ADB is helping the Philippines protect its vast upper river basins by improving watershed management. The project covers the Chico River Basin in northern Luzon, Wahig–Inabanga in central Visayas, and Lake Lanao Basin and Upper Bukidnon River Basin, both in the Mindanao region. The project supports reforestation, climate change mitigation, and livelihood measures. This web page in adb.org contains a collection of documents produced under this project, including resettlement and environmental safeguards documents.

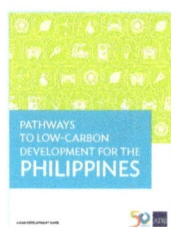

***Pathways to Low-Carbon Development for the Philippines* (2017).** This study assesses how the Philippines can take a low-carbon pathway by drawing on detailed modeling of the power, residential, and transport sectors. It identifies low-carbon development options that can be deployed at approximately zero net cost to reduce energy sector greenhouse gas emissions by 70% by 2050. With energy use levels still low, the country has an opportunity to follow a low-carbon development trajectory if action is taken soon.

Status of Climate Finance in the Philippines (2015). This presentation was made at the Training Workshop on Corruption Risks and Anti-Corruption Strategies in Climate Financing, held in May 2015 at ADB. It discusses the Philippines' position on climate change, the country's comprehensive climate change agenda, and a special government-administered national climate fund designed to support local efforts in climate change adaptation.

Good Governance and Inclusive Finance

Good Governance

Good governance and the rule of law are government priorities comprising one of the main chapters of the *Philippine Development Plan, 2011–2016*. Good governance is also a long-established theme of ADB's partnership with the Philippines. The 2011–2016 CPS aimed to strengthen governance and reduce corruption at country, sector, and project levels. Two significant aspects of this work are (i) building local government capacity for revenue generation, planning, budgeting, and financial management; and (ii) supporting a more efficient delivery of public sector resources (including ADB financing).

Local government reform and fiscal decentralization have been a major focus of ADB assistance. Knowledge solutions were critical in supporting the reform process. These solutions include an intensive knowledge transfer initiative, the TA for the Support to Local Government Revenue Generation and Land Administration Reforms (ADB 2011e). This project—which aimed at strengthening local government land management and administration—delivered capacity development on e-government systems, land valuation, tax compliance and valuation; and initiated planning for land use, disaster risk management, and climate change adaptation. Good practice models for land valuation were developed and adopted for national roll out, and a capacity development plan for the Bureau of Local Government Finance was completed. A working paper on local good governance (ADB 2015d) aimed to stimulate discussion on innovative future interventions for a wider and more substantial impact of local good governance.

Summaries of Selected Knowledge Products

Participatory Budgeting in the Philippines (2017). Bottom-up budgeting served as the foundation to identify key challenges and the possible means of addressing issues such as how to strengthen local governance and service delivery in the Philippine government. This presentation shares what worked, what did not, and recommended actions for improving the approach. This was presented by the Department of the Interior and Local Government at the workshop on Open Government for Improving Public Services in Asia, held in August 2017 at ADB.

***Taxing Properties and Managing Land: The Many Pathways on a Long Journey in the Philippines* (2016).** This case study summarizes lessons and good practices from the TA for the Support to Local Government Revenue Generation and Land Administration Reforms (page 12), and its predecessor, the AusAID-financed Innovation Support Fund. It was presented and discussed at the "New Ideas in Governance" event held in ADB in 2016. These projects demonstrate that reforms are doable at the local level when local and national governments are committed and working in partnership, with development partner support providing momentum and rigor.

***Building Modern Land Administration Systems* (2015).** This brief describes how an ADB TA improved land administration services and enhanced revenues in five participating LGUs. The brief emphasizes the importance of effective land administration in economic growth, environmental management, and good governance. It notes that in the Philippines, inadequate ownership information weakens security of tenure, opens the system to abuse, and impacts performance across both private and public sectors. The brief also recognizes the progress achieved through national initiatives and describes how the project piloted land administration improvements at the local level.

Corporate Governance

Good governance is not only a public sector issue. Through a regional TA project (ADB 2010b), ADB supported the advances in private sector governance across the Association of Southeast Asian Nations (ASEAN) member countries. This work highlighted the strong progress made in the Philippines on corporate governance, resulting in valuable knowledge products and services that demonstrate and disseminate good practice. To enhance the integration of the region's capital markets, the TA supported the ASEAN Capital Market Forum. The aim was to develop and implement harmonized corporate governance scorecards—based on the Organisation for Economic Co-operation and Development (OECD) guidelines—for assessing the status of publicly listed companies in member countries. Based on these assessments, the ASEAN Capital Market Forum, with support from ADB, produced annual country reports on corporate governance (ADB 2014f). In 2014, it held a milestone regional conference on this subject in Manila. The conference reviewed the progress on scorecard assessments and launched the Philippine Corporate Governance Blueprint (Building a Stronger Corporate Governance Framework 2015), a detailed plan for improving corporate governance in the country over the next 5 years.

Summaries of Selected Knowledge Products

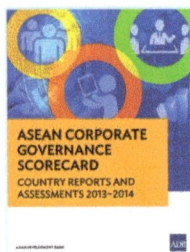

ASEAN Corporate Governance Scorecard: Country Reports and Assessments, 2013–2014 (2014). The ASEAN Corporate Governance Scorecard is a harmonized approach to measuring progress in corporate governance across the ASEAN member countries. This assessment approach covers five areas: (i) rights of shareholders, (ii) equitable treatment of shareholders, (iii) role of stakeholders, (iv) transparency and disclosure, and (v) responsibilities of the board. The report assesses 529 publicly listed companies, including 94 from the Philippines. Overall, a 19% improvement in mean total scores was noted over the previous year. The scores of the top 100 Philippine companies improved, but the report notes the need for better disclosure of company information.

ASEAN Corporate Governance Scorecard: Country Reports and Assessments, 2015 (2017). In this fourth edition of the ASEAN Corporate Governance initiative of ADB and the ASEAN Capital Markets Forum, over 500 top publicly listed companies from six ASEAN countries were assessed. In-depth analysis of each country, including rights of shareholders, equitable treatment of shareholders, role of stakeholders, disclosure and transparency, and responsibilities of the board are discussed.

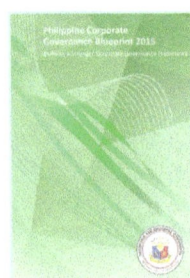

Philippine Corporate Governance Blueprint 2015: Building a Stronger Corporate Governance Framework. This is a road map for corporate governance, developed by the Philippine Securities and Exchange Commission and supported by ADB. The document provides guidance for all Philippine corporations on best practice as set out in the ASEAN Corporate Governance Framework. The road map summarizes the latest assessment of corporate governance in the Philippines. It also presents detailed recommendations for improving the governance framework, such as (i) providing adequate authority, capacity, and resources to the Securities and Exchange Commission; (ii) updating relevant laws and regulations; (iii) improving the regulation of external auditors; (iv) launching stock exchange initiatives; (v) formulating a comprehensive corporate governance strategy; (vi) rationalizing reporting requirements; (vii) finding a more efficient resolution of capital market legal cases; and (viii) harmonizing the rules of regulatory agencies.

Inclusive Finance

Ensuring that low-cost financial services reach the poor is a worldwide issue of growing importance. The Government of the Philippines, with the support of ADB and other development partners, has been striving to improve the enabling environment for inclusive financial services. The country is now one of the leading promoters of microinsurance in the region. Knowledge solutions played an important role, through the outputs of a Japan Fund for Poverty Reduction-funded TA project, which aimed to expand the microinsurance market in the Philippines. The Developing Microinsurance Project (ADB 2008) supported the creation of a regulatory framework and national strategy for microinsurance in the country. It also prepared a detailed assessment of microinsurance in the Philippines (ADB 2013j), concluding with a national conference in September 2012 that showcased its progress and identified remaining issues and gaps to be addressed. An ADB working paper explores another crucial aspect of inclusive finance—lending to micro, small, and medium-sized enterprises (MSMEs). The paper provides a unique assessment of the government's mandatory Magna Carta program and proposes ways for improving lending to this sector (ADB 2015e).

Summaries of Selected Knowledge Products

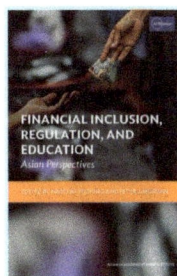

***Financial Inclusion, Regulation, and Education: Asian Perspectives* (2017)**. This book showcases successful experiences of some developed countries in providing low-income households and small firms with access to financial services while providing financial literacy, financial education programs, and financial regulatory frameworks. Lessons drawn from these developed countries can be adopted by Asian emerging economies. The book also identifies policies that can improve financial access of low-income households and small firms while maintaining financial stability. The studies cover the experiences of Bangladesh, Germany, India, Indonesia, the Philippines, Sri Lanka, Thailand, and the United Kingdom.

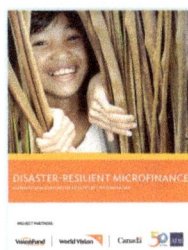

***Disaster-Resilient Microfinance: Learning from Communities Affected by Typhoon Haiyan* (2016)**. The report presents the experiences, analyses, and conclusions of VisionFund International and their Philippine microfinance firm, the Community Economic Ventures Incorporated. This analysis follows the economic recovery of over 4,000 client households severely affected by typhoon Haiyan/Yolanda over the 18 months following the calamity. It also seeks to derive recommendations for future financial disaster risk management solutions.

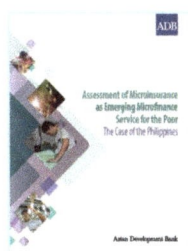

***Assessment of Microinsurance as Emerging Microfinance Service for the Poor—The Case of the Philippines* (2013)**. This study provides guidance on developing microinsurance as a pro-poor microfinance service in ADB DMCs based on lessons from the Developing Microinsurance Project in the Philippines. The document assesses the country's microinsurance sector—covering the Philippine insurance industry, government policy thrusts, and sector strategy. It also details the history of microfinance in the country and its regulatory, commercial, and awareness issues. The main lessons, according to the study, are the (i) importance of establishing an appropriate policy and regulatory environment; (ii) government's ownership and championing of reform measures; (iii) technical working groups, including government and private sector, being effective tools in the reform process; (iv) regulations that facilitate and follow market development; and (v) government's active role in implementation, which facilitates donor coordination.

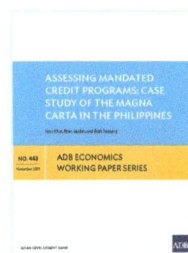

***Assessing Mandated Credit Programs: Case Study of the Magna Carta in the Philippines* (2015).** This paper examines the Magna Carta Law in the Philippines, which mandates banks to allocate 2% of their total loan portfolios to medium-sized firms and 8% to micro and small firms. Three findings are highlighted. First, although total lending to micro, small, and medium-sized enterprises (MSMEs) grew slightly, MSME loan shares declined drastically from 30.0% (2002) to 16.4% (2010). Second, there was a sharp rise in noncompliance after loan targets increased in 2008. Third, there is increased heterogeneity in optimal loan portfolio across banks. Most surprising is the total MSME lending by rural and cooperative banks, which declined since 2008. Abolishing the Magna Carta target for medium-sized enterprise loans would most likely yield little adverse effects.

Education, Employment, and Social Protection

Education and Employment

The government has taken bold steps to improve education in the Philippines. It expanded basic education to cover 12 years starting from kindergarten, from the previous 10 years, and revised the elementary curriculum. However, ADB assessments of the sector emphasize that gaps in the quality of basic education continue to hinder poverty reduction and inclusive growth. While female enrollment and performance are high, gender advantages do not carry through to the labor market. During the 2011–2016 CPS, a number of knowledge-focused TAs sought to address some of these gaps.

The successful Computer Access Mentorship Program (ADB 2010c) delivered an online training program for elementary teachers to improve the teaching of reading. It expanded access to the program by setting up computers in several locations nationwide where teachers could access the online program and gain skills. The TA project, Strengthening Knowledge-Based Economic and Social Development (ADB 2012h), sought to align higher education programs with the needs of employers by enhancing, digitizing, and making interactive industry-designed courses on management, business, technology, and other topics.

The Employment Facilitation for Inclusive Growth (ADB 2013k) was a significant initiative that supported the Department of Labor and Employment (DOLE) in enhancing the employability of at-risk youths through policy reform and the JobStart Philippines Program. This program provided the youth with career guidance and employment coaching, along with information on local labor market conditions and career assessments. Key knowledge solutions included (i) capacity building of DOLE staff on labor policy and labor program monitoring, (ii) a national labor policy conference, and (iii) knowledge products to support the implementation of JobStart Philippines.

While the Philippines has a strong record in promoting and protecting gender equity in education and employment, a number of challenges remain, particularly on women's access to training, resources, and services needed to participate fully in the labor market. Two regional ADB studies with strong focus on the Philippines provided policy makers with valuable knowledge and guidance on this issue. The TA, Promoting Gender Equality in the Labor Market for More Inclusive Growth (ADB 2010d) included an in-depth study on how labor market reform could expand opportunities for women. A follow-up national workshop—in collaboration with the International Labour Organization (ILO)—reviewed and discussed the findings of the study. A further research study (ADB 2013l) looked into the impact of the global economic crisis on migrant workers and their families with a specific gender perspective. This revealed an increasing feminization of migration and significant gender differences in the impacts of the global crisis on migrant labor, which must be taken into account in policy development.

Summaries of Selected Knowledge Products

Reducing Youth Not in Employment, Education, or Training through JobStart Philippines (2018). This brief outlines the key points of this project. Youth that are not in employment, education, or training and the slow school-to-work transition is a challenge in the Philippines. In 2013, one in four young Filipinos (aged 15–24) were not in employment, education, or training. During 2014–2015, the DOLE piloted the JobStart Philippines Program in four LGUs. The program assisted young Filipinos in starting their careers through formal or technical training to enhance their skills and help them better respond to the demands of the job market, by providing them with better integration opportunities into productive employment. This brief was released in January 2018, but content preparation was completed in 2017.

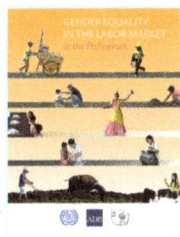

Gender Equality in the Labor Market in the Philippines (2013). This report analyzes gender equality in the labor market and gender-related policies and legislation in the Philippines and concludes with recommendations to promote gender equality. In the Philippines, the estimated proportion of women's annual earnings to men's annual earnings is less than 60%. Also, employment growth alone is not a sufficient basis for assessing whether there is inclusive growth. Gender inequality in the labor market is ascertained in this report by looking at the following seven gender gaps (or deficits for women): (i) labor force participation, (ii) human capital, (iii) unpaid domestic and care work burden, (iv) vulnerable employment, (v) wage employment, (vi) decent work, and (vii) social protection. Despite a variety of gender-responsive legal and policy initiatives, an assessment of the labor market in the Philippines reveals that although some gender gaps have been reduced, women still suffer from persistent gender deficits.

Computer Access Mentorship Program: Public–Private Partnership for Enhancing Education Quality (2013). This TA consultant's report describes the activities of *Sa Aklat Sisikat* Foundation in developing and providing access when it implemented this ADB TA technology-driven training program, which aimed to improve the teaching of reading in public schools through online courses for teachers. The report includes the results of a baseline survey, a report on the usage of the online training program, and an evaluation of the program.

Social Protection

In 2008, the government launched the *Pantawid Pamilyang Pilipino* Program, a social protection initiative that provides cash transfers to poor households, with the condition that they avail of maternal health services and keep their children in school. ADB has been a strong partner in the development of this program. Through the Social Protection Support Project (ADB 2010e), ADB delivered knowledge solutions that supported the government in strengthening and reforming the program. A landmark review and policy brief—*After Five Years of Pantawid, What Next?* (PIDS 2013)—was based on an extensive evaluation exercise that examined the experiences in implementing the program and the potential for extending the benefits to families beyond the original 5-year target period. Additional work under the Social Protection Support Project assisted the improvement and expansion of the program, which included (i) a framework for capacity development, (ii) studies on gender issues and monitoring a pilot for indigenous peoples, and (iii) a demand-led knowledge support to government during the reform process.

Another pillar of the government's social protection program is the community-driven development (CDD) approach. Over the last 15 years, both government and development partners have jointly reduced poverty and achieved far-reaching development impact in the Philippines using this approach (ADB 2013n). Based on this positive experience, the Department of Social Welfare and Development (DSWD) launched in 2013 the National Community-Driven Development Program to scale up its flagship CDD initiative—the *Kapit-Bisig Laban sa Kahirapan* Comprehensive and Integrated Delivery of Social Services (KALAHI-CIDSS). An ADB TA supported the conceptualization and design of the program (ADB 2012i) and helped prepare a series of key policy notes on LGU engagement toward integrating CDD into the LGU systems. All these assisted the DSWD in designing local counterpart contributions for the national program. A preparatory analysis for ADB loan assistance to the KALAHI-CIDSS program (ADB 2013o) was done under the TA, which eventually supported the recovery, reconstruction, and poverty reduction in areas affected by typhoon Haiyan/Yolanda.

Summaries of Selected Knowledge Products

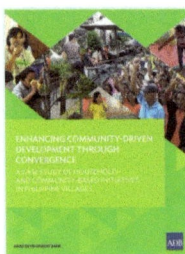

Enhancing Community-Driven Development through Convergence: A Case Study of Household- and Community-Based Initiatives in Philippine Villages (2016). The study looks at the interactions among the three major development assistance programs implemented by the DSWD—KALAHI-CIDSS National CDD Program, *Pantawid Pamilyang Pilipino* Program, and Sustainable Livelihood Program. The study also assesses the coordination among DSWD programs and the development interventions of other national government agencies.

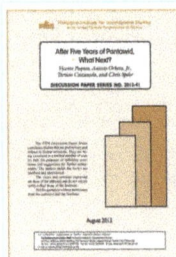

After Five Years of Pantawid, What Next? A Policy Brief for the Department of Social Welfare and Development (2013). This policy brief supported the government's decision in extending the *Pantawid Pamilyang Pilipino* Program—which provides conditional cash transfers (CCTs) to poor families for improving the health, nutrition, and education of children. The brief recommends the extension of CCT benefits based on five arguments: (i) the program continues to be relevant to the country's development effort, (ii) CCT is a valuable instrument for poverty reduction, (iii) extension would lead to greater welfare impacts for the poor, (iv) extension would allow time to develop a transition strategy, and (v) grants for secondary education could improve enrollment that will result in increased earnings of beneficiaries. The brief concludes that extending the benefits would (i) be economically and socially beneficial, (ii) allow the government time to develop a transition promotion strategy, (iii) strengthen the impact of the program, and (iv) enable the government to undertake policy reforms needed to expand job opportunities.

The KALAHI-CIDSS Project in the Philippines: Sharing Knowledge on Community-Driven Development (2012). This report assesses the KALAHI-CIDSS project in the Philippines to determine its contribution in improving service delivery and governance in the beneficiary communities. KALAHI-CIDSS was found to be effective in (i) facilitating broad-based participation of community residents, (ii) addressing local priorities, (iii) delivering basic services to intended beneficiaries, and (iv) creating a venue for LGU officials to collaborate with beneficiaries in managing the subprojects. The project created positive effects on the income and non-income dimensions of poverty. It is valued highly by recipient communities, participating local governments, and development partners.

Improving Local Service Delivery through Community-Driven Development Approach (2013). Coauthored by an ADB staff, this paper was presented at an international conference organized by the Eastern Regional Organization for Public Administration in Tokyo in October 2013, with a revised version published in the *Asian Review of Public Administration*. It discusses CDD as an effective approach in the delivery of basic services, as it is more responsive to people's needs. The paper reviews the literature on local service delivery and outlines factors that challenge it, tracing concepts from public choice theory, political economy, and decentralization. It also discusses the principles and experiences of CDD in the Philippines. Drawing from experiences within and outside the country, the paper summarizes the evidence-backed benefits of CDD, as follows: (i) investments in basic community infrastructure and services reflect the expressed needs of the people, (ii) full sharing of financial information is promoted, (iii) poorest localities are well targeted, (iv) community projects enjoy economies of scale, (v) community projects show good economic rates of return, (vi) risks from corruption are reduced, (vii) costs of subprojects are lowered, (viii) projects are of good quality and have sustained operations and maintenance, and (ix) CDD enhances the functions of local planning councils. The paper has been used and cited in policy dialogues with government counterparts in the Philippines, particularly in strengthening the institutional mechanisms for mainstreaming CDD approaches in local governance.

Regional Cooperation and Integration

The ASEAN Economic Community

ADB support to regional cooperation in Southeast Asia has grown steadily in recent decades. Support includes assistance to activities of the subregional groups, such as the Brunei Darussalam–Indonesia–Malaysia–Philippines East ASEAN Growth Area (BIMP-EAGA) and the Indonesia–Malaysia–Thailand Growth Triangle. The idea of establishing an ASEAN Economic Community (AEC) was first raised at the ASEAN Summit in Phnom Penh in 2002. A detailed blueprint and plan of action for achieving this community by 2015 were adopted during the ASEAN Summit in Singapore in 2007. Since the initiative began, ADB has supported the ASEAN's economic and financial integration efforts through research, monitoring, and knowledge and advisory work toward the goal of establishing the AEC. As the 2015 deadline approached, the ASEAN Secretariat requested ADB to do an analysis of the barriers and impediments to realizing the AEC. A series of nine studies—carried out under an ADB TA (ADB 2010f) culminated in a milestone knowledge product on AEC's progress (Das et al. 2013) that was disseminated regionwide, while another published working paper (ADB 2015f) updated this analysis and reviewed the remaining challenges.

Summary of a Selected Knowledge Product

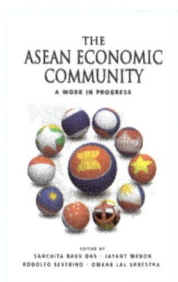

***The ASEAN Economic Community: A Work in Progress* (2013).** This study analyzes the barriers and impediments to realizing an ASEAN Economic Community (AEC) by the target date of 2015. The study reviews the concept of ASEAN as an economic community. It discusses progress in key areas of economic integration, particularly tariff liberalization, the investment climate, competition and intellectual property laws, subregional zones, free trade agreements, dispute settlement systems, and the institutional framework. The contributing experts concluded that it would be very difficult to achieve the AEC by 2015 in terms of commitments specified in the AEC Blueprint. Progress has been made in lowering tariffs, but nontariff barriers remain, liberalization of trade in services has been slow, and regional institutions remain weak. A sudden transformation of the ASEAN is unlikely, and the 2015 target should be regarded more as a measure of work in progress, but momentum toward the commitments must be maintained to ensure that the credibility of the vision is not lost. This study provided valuable analyses for member countries working toward the AEC, and for development partners supporting them in key areas of economic integration.

Regional Environmental Management

The livelihood of millions of Filipinos depends on the natural resources and ecosystem services provided by coral reefs. In 2007, the Philippines joined the six-country multilateral Coral Triangle Initiative (CTI), a major program that aims to safeguard the region's marine and coastal resources. Since the launch of the CTI Regional Plan of Action in 2009 (CTI 2009), ADB has been a key partner in the initiative, providing both technical and financial support across the six member countries including the Philippines. Knowledge management was an early focus of ADB assistance through a regional TA that aimed to strengthen regional cooperation on coastal marine resources (ADB 2009c). Baseline resource assessments under this TA resulted in knowledge products on the state of the Coral Triangle, both regionally and in the Philippines, which continue to inform the implementation of the initiative (ADB, CTI, and GEF 2014a, 2014b). The TA also made a detailed study on the economics of fisheries and aquaculture in the Coral Triangle, including numerous case studies drawn from the Philippines (ADB, Government of Australia, CTI, and GEF 2014). Another highly valued knowledge solution provided a costing of the CTI Philippine plan of action with estimates of investment needs, long-term recurrent costs, and likely gaps in funding (CTI 2015).

Summaries of Selected Knowledge Products

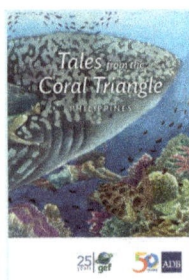

***Tales from the Coral Triangle: Philippines* (2016).** These 10 winning entries from the "Our Seas" story writing contest for high school students in Palawan, Philippines employ fantasy, humor, and drama to highlight the importance of protecting the ocean. The stories demonstrate the young authors' keen awareness of the interconnection between people and the environment, and the vital role of conservation and environmental protection in ensuring the well-being of the human race.

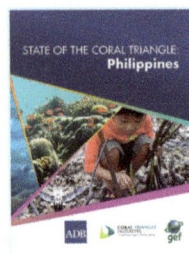

***State of the Coral Triangle: Philippines* (2014).** This report describes the condition of coastal ecosystems in the Philippines, paying particular attention to exploited resources, especially fisheries. The report highlights the current main threats to the marine ecosystem and notes that while destructive fishing practices have decreased, other threats like coastal development, pollution, sedimentation, and overfishing have intensified. The consolidation of all available information on the state of the country's coastal and marine resources has been highly valuable for policy makers and development partners as this directly contributed to the preparation and implementation of ADB's technical assistance support to the CTI.

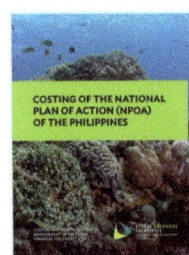

***Costing of the National Plan of Action of the Philippines*, 2015.** This report outlines the costs of implementing the Philippines' national plan of action (NPOA) under the CTI and presents estimates of the necessary investments, funding gaps, and long-term recurrent costs. It reviews the status of NPOA implementation, summarizing the progress in achieving the CTI goals, and profiling projects that are currently contributing to implementation. The report recommends a target-setting exercise for NPOA to (i) identify activities that can be absorbed by existing budget allocations for national and local agencies, (ii) develop proposals for under/unfunded actions, (iii) determine and pilot modalities for sustainable financing, and (iv) ensure policy support for sustainable finance modalities.

Trade Facilitation in Brunei Darussalam–Indonesia–Malaysia–Philippines East ASEAN Growth Area

The Brunei Darussalam–Indonesia–Malaysia–Philippines East ASEAN Growth Area (BIMP-EAGA) was formed in 1994 to address development gaps across and within its member countries. ADB has supported BIMP-EAGA since its inception and, given its importance in achieving economic integration, trade facilitation featured strongly in the TA. ADB supported the preparation of the BIMP-EAGA Vision 2025 (BEV 2025), which was adopted by the leaders of Brunei Darussalam, Indonesia, Malaysia, and the Philippines at the 12th BIMP-EAGA Summit on 29 April 2017 in Manila, Philippines.

ADB provided a TA to support BIMP-EAGA's efforts to harmonize customs, immigration, quarantine, and security rules, regulations, and procedures in major ports and land border crossings. ADB also completed a study on Land Transport Facilitation, which provided recommendations for improving the implementation of BIMP-EAGA's memoranda of understanding in land transport in the areas of insurance, transit, authorized economic operators, and common permits to cross borders. Two studies—Economic Corridors: Business Perceptions about the Investment Climate and Investment Opportunities in Corridor Value Chains—were also completed in 2017.

Summaries of Selected Knowledge Products

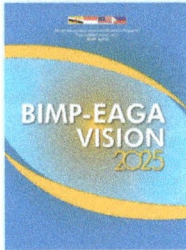

BIMP-EAGA Vision 2025 (2017). The BIMP-EAGA 2025 vision is a "Resilient, Inclusive, Sustainable and Economically competitive (R.I.S.E.) BIMP-EAGA to narrow development gap." Its pipeline of priority infrastructure projects is estimated at $21 billion. ADB will provide technical and financial support and will closely collaborate with BIMP-EAGA working groups, clusters, the BIMP-EAGA Facilitation Center, and other subregional mechanisms to implement this vision.

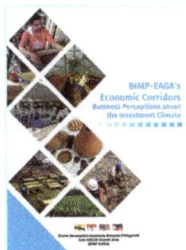

BIMP-EAGA'S Economic Corridors: Business Perceptions about the Investment Climate (2017). This study examines the investment climate impacting on decisions to invest in the economic corridors of BIMP-EAGA. Businesses identified the following as the key factors that affect their investment decisions in BIMP-EAGA's corridors: (i) complementarities in cross-border production activities and services, (ii) investment incentives, (iii) hard and soft infrastructure, (iv) the regulatory environment, (v) governance, and (vi) other issues affecting cross-border investments.

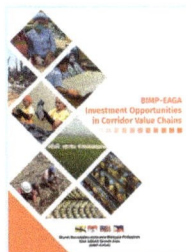

BIMP-EAGA Investment Opportunities in Corridor Value Chains (2017). Cross-border production sharing has advantages over global value chains because they offer proximity to factor inputs and markets. For BIMP-EAGA, corridor provinces and states build on established relations from social, cultural, and historical ties in the areas. This study examines potential investment opportunities for cross-border value chains in the economic corridors of BIMP-EAGA: (i) the West Borneo Economic Corridor, covering Brunei Darussalam, West Kalimantan in Indonesia, and Sabah and Sarawak in Malaysia; and (ii) the Greater Sulu–Sulawesi Economic Corridor, a maritime corridor covering North Sulawesi in Indonesia, Sabah in Malaysia, and the Mindanao island group and Palawan in the Philippines.

3 Pursuing the Knowledge Agenda

Under the latest Country Partnership Strategy: Philippines, 2018–2023—High and Inclusive Growth, ADB's operational focus was categorized under three pillars—accelerating infrastructure and long-term investments, promoting local economic development, and investing in people. This is being pursued through timely support on key policy reforms, targeted institutional capacity development, and financing catalytic investments that promote high and inclusive growth. Knowledge work maintained its focus on analytical and advisory support for (i) preparing lending operations, capacity development, gathering lessons learned from monitoring and evaluation of operations; and (ii) developing and initiating government reform initiatives and innovations.

Up until 2020, the Philippines enjoyed a strong gross domestic product (GDP) growth and favorable macroeconomic fundamentals, with national development plans and priorities more focused on inclusive growth. The government made a stronger commitment to good governance and placed greater emphasis on results. Good progress was also achieved in key areas of the country where increased development support is needed. The passage of the Bangsamoro Organic Law in 2018, for instance, has led to the creation of the Bangsamoro Autonomous Region in Muslim Mindanao, fueling renewed hope for accelerating development in Mindanao and achieving the government's goal of inclusive growth particularly in that region.

Despite these gains, the country continues to struggle with high vulnerability to widespread social and economic damage from natural disasters, extreme weather events, and more recently, pandemics such as the coronavirus disease (COVID-19). Measures to contain the spread of the COVID-19 virus resulted in significant costs to the economy similar to what was seen globally—a deep contraction in GDP, a record rise in unemployment, and lost income opportunities for millions of Filipino families. In February 2021, the National Economic and Development Authority (NEDA) launched its updated Philippine Development Plan, 2017–2022, a result of regional, national, and public consultations with stakeholders to lay down the foundation for inclusive growth, resilient society, and a globally competitive knowledge economy that remains responsive to shifting priorities in the transition to the new normal. The updated plan responds to the challenges brought by the COVID-19 pandemic and provides strategies for the country's economic recovery. Amid this changing landscape, the country's knowledge needs are also evolving into a combination of themes that include support for the country's recovery from emerging environmental, economic, social, and health-related challenges.

In 2020, ADB sought to recalibrate its country knowledge program to better align with the country's needs. A strategic approach to identify relevant knowledge support was launched to (i) achieve the long-term objectives laid out in AmBisyon Natin 2040, (ii) underpin ADB's operations and ensure close linkage to the country partnership strategy (CPS), and (iii) revisit current and future knowledge needs in view of the COVID-19 pandemic. This process will result in a new Country Knowledge Program (CKP) for 2021–2022 which will outline the agreed knowledge products and services for delivery for those years. The CKP is demand driven and will support knowledge generation in areas that are relevant to the Philippines' development priorities. This approach avoids fragmentation of knowledge services away from evolving priorities and strengthens the contribution of knowledge to the country's development. Aligning ADB's knowledge resources with the Philippines' knowledge demands will form part of ADB's annual country programming exercise with the government.

Figure 4: ADB's Updated Country Knowledge Approach for the Philippines

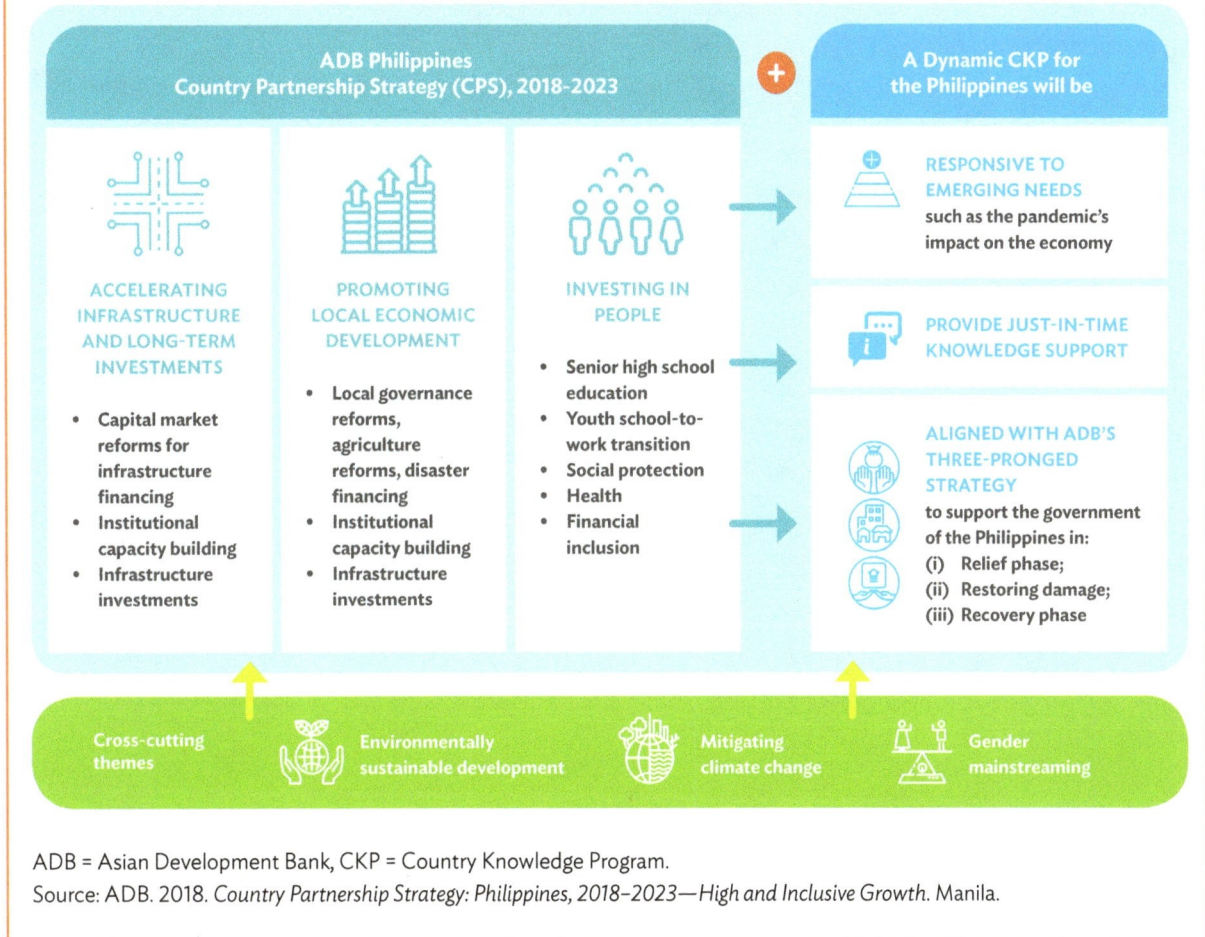

ADB Philippines Country Partnership Strategy (CPS), 2018-2023

+

A Dynamic CKP for the Philippines will be

ACCELERATING INFRASTRUCTURE AND LONG-TERM INVESTMENTS

- Capital market reforms for infrastructure financing
- Institutional capacity building
- Infrastructure investments

PROMOTING LOCAL ECONOMIC DEVELOPMENT

- Local governance reforms, agriculture reforms, disaster financing
- Institutional capacity building
- Infrastructure investments

INVESTING IN PEOPLE

- Senior high school education
- Youth school-to-work transition
- Social protection
- Health
- Financial inclusion

RESPONSIVE TO EMERGING NEEDS such as the pandemic's impact on the economy

PROVIDE JUST-IN-TIME KNOWLEDGE SUPPORT

ALIGNED WITH ADB'S THREE-PRONGED STRATEGY to support the government of the Philippines in:
(i) Relief phase;
(ii) Restoring damage;
(iii) Recovery phase

Cross-cutting themes — Environmentally sustainable development — Mitigating climate change — Gender mainstreaming

ADB = Asian Development Bank, CKP = Country Knowledge Program.
Source: ADB. 2018. *Country Partnership Strategy: Philippines, 2018–2023—High and Inclusive Growth.* Manila.

Areas of Collaboration with Partners

ADB will work closely with development partners and local stakeholders to enhance the relevance and impact of its knowledge support. As the lead development partner in the Philippines, ADB will support the closer coordination of sector and thematic analysis, policy dialogue, and sector reforms.

The CKP raises ADB's collaboration with government agencies on knowledge to a new level, with a knowledge needs assessment to be conducted to ensure alignment of the identified needs to government priorities and ADB's operations before developing the knowledge product or solution. On 4–8 February 2021, ADB's Philippines Country Office and the Knowledge Advisory Services Center of the Sustainable Development and Climate Change Department hosted a series of virtual CKP consultations, which brought together more than 200 representatives from 34 government departments and agencies to identify knowledge products and services for possible joint collaboration in 2021 and 2022.

Resource Allocation

ADB staff will be at the forefront of support to the Philippines' knowledge needs and the strategic directions of the CKP. Focal persons will be identified in ADB and the partner government agency tasked to monitor the implementation of the identified knowledge product or solution. The CKP will incorporate the resources allocated, including through TA, for project preparation and implementation, capacity development, and knowledge work, as guided by the Country Operations Business Plan, 2021–2023.

Selected Knowledge Products and Services, Philippines, 2012–2017

Type	Category	Title	Date	Coverage
Economic Development and Poverty Reduction				
Book	EDP	Philippines Country Chapter, Asian Development Outlook	2012–2017 annually	PHI
Report	EDP	Philippines Country Chapter, Asian Development Outlook Update	2012–2017 annually	PHI
Strategy	EDP	AmBisyon Natin 2040	2017	PHI
Presentation	EDP	Capacity Development for Growth and Poverty Reduction in Mindanao and Bangsamoro: A Medium- to Long-Term Approach	2017	PHI
Working Paper	EDP	Analytical Tools for Measuring Poverty Dynamics: An Application Using Panel Data in the Philippines	2016	PHI
Report	EDP	ADB Support for Inclusive Growth	2014	Asia/Pacific
Book	EDP	The Environments of the Poor in Southeast Asia, East Asia, and the Pacific	2014	Asia/Pacific
Report	EDP	Urban Poverty in Asia	2014	Asia/PHI
Book	EDP	Asia Rising: Growth and Resilience in an Uncertain Global Economy	2013	Asia/PHI
Working Paper	EDP	Leveraging Service Sector Growth in the Philippines	2013	PHI
Working Paper	EDP	The Middle-Income Trap: Issues for Members of the Association of South East Asian Nations	2013	SEA
Working Paper	EDP	Do Imports Fall More than Exports Especially During Crises? Evidence from Selected Asian Economies	2012	SEA
Report	EDP	Taking the Right Road to Inclusive Growth: Industrial Upgrading and Diversification in the Philippines	2012	PHI
Working Paper	EDP	The Service Sector in Asia: Is It an Engine of Growth?	2012	Asia/PHI
Working Paper	EDP	Tracking the Middle-Income Trap: What is it, Who is in it, and Why? Part 2	2012	Asia/PHI
Sustainable and Climate-Resilient Infrastructure				
Working Paper	ST	Scaling Up Infrastructure Investment in the Philippines: Role of Public–Private Partnership and Issues	2017	PHI
Working Paper	ST	The Impact of Improved Transport Connectivity on Income, Education, and Health: The Case of the Roll-On/Roll-Off System in the Philippines	2017	PHI

continued on next page

Table *continued*

Type	Category	Title	Date	Coverage
Report	ST	Davao Sustainable Urban Transport Project: Final Report	2015	PHI
Brief	ST	Infrastructure Asset Management: Can the Canadian Municipal Experience Help Inform Better Practices in Southeast Asia?	2015	PHI
Working Paper	ST	The "Highway Effect" on Public Finance: Case of the STAR Highway in the Philippines	2015	PHI
Capacity Development	ST	Train-the-Trainer Workshop on Road Safety in ASEAN Countries	2015	Asia/PHI
Brief	ST	Upgrading the Cebu International Passenger Terminal in the Philippines	2015	PHI
Capacity Development	ST	Capacity Development Program for Davao City Technical Officers	2013	PHI
Event	ST	Davao City Transport Summit	2013	PHI
Event	ST	Forums on Comprehensive Public Transport Reform Strategy for Davao City	2013	PHI
Event	ST	Forums on Sustainable Urban Transport Project	2013	PHI
Video	ST	New Electric Vehicles: First Step Towards Green Transportation Revolution in Philippines	2013	PHI
Report	ST	Recent Trends in Road Asset Management and Case Studies	2013	PHI/MLD/NZL
Event	ST	Workshop with Local Government Officials on Effective Public Transport Reform	2013	PHI
Report	ST	Compendium of Transport Operations in Southeast Asia	2012	SEA
Manual/Guide	ST	Developing Public–Private Partnerships in Local Infrastructure and Development Projects: A PPP Manual for Local Government Units	2012	PHI
Event	ST	New Mobility Mapping Activity	2012	PHI
Sector Assessment	ST	Philippines: Transport Sector Assessment, Strategy, and Road Map	2012	PHI
Urban Infrastructure				
Sector Assessment	URB	Republic of the Philippines: National Urban Assessment	2014	PHI
Report	URB	Urban Metabolism of Six Asian Cities	2014	Asia/PHI
Book	URB	Green Cities	2012	Asia/PHI
Manual/Guide	URB	Materials Recovery Facility Toolkit	2012	PHI
Sector Assessment	URB	Philippines: Urban Sector Assessment Strategy and Road Map	2012	PHI
Brief	URB	Project Impact: Mindanao Basic Urban Services Sector Project Improves Urban Facilities	2012	PHI

continued on next page

Table *continued*

Type	Category	Title	Date	Coverage
Water and Sanitation				
Manual/Guide	WAT	A Guide to Sanitation Safety Planning in the Philippines	2016	PHI
Report	WAT	NARBO: A Decade of Achievements (2004–2014)–Promoting IWRM and Improving Water Governance	2015	PHI
Book	WAT	From Toilets to Rivers: Experiences, New Opportunities, and Innovative Solutions	2014	Asia/PHI
Book	WAT	Tap Secrets: The Manila Water Story	2014	PHI
Manual/Guide	WAT	Urban Water Supply and Sanitation in Southeast Asia: A Guide to Good Practice	2014	SEA
Brief	WAT	Water Operators Partnerships Case Study: Twinning Khulna WASA and Maynilad	2014	PHI
Event	WAT	Presentation: Supporting Water Operators Partnerships in Asia and the Pacific	2013	Asia/Pacific
Sector Assessment	WAT	Water Supply and Sanitation Sector Assessment and Road Map	2013	PHI
Book	WAT	Good Practices in Urban Water Management: Decoding Good Practices for a Successful Future	2012	Asia/PHI
Energy Infrastructure				
Report	ENE	Wave Energy Conversion and Ocean Thermal Energy Conversion Potential in Developing Countries	2015	Asia/PHI
Book	ENE	Asian Development Outlook 2013 Update: Asia's Energy Challenge	2013	Asia/Pacific
Book	ENE	Energy Outlook for Asia and the Pacific	2013	Asia/Pacific
Book	ENE	Energy Statistics in Asia and the Pacific	2013	Asia/Pacific
Brief	ENE	Maximizing Access to Energy for the Poor in Developing Asia	2013	Asia/PHI
Report	ENE	Same Energy, More Power: Accelerating Energy Efficiency in Asia	2013	Asia/PHI
Environment, Climate Change, and Disaster Risk Management				
Website	ENV	Typhoon Haiyan: ADB's Response	Ongoing	PHI
Website	ENV	Integrated Natural Resources and Environmental Management Project—Documents	Ongoing	PHI
Report	ENV	Pathways to Low-Carbon Development for the Philippines	2017	PHI
Brief	ENV	Lessons from Community-Led Actions for Strengthening Disaster Resilience: A Case from the Philippines	2017	
Book	ENV	Tales from the Coral Triangle: Philippines	2016	
Report	ENV	Asia Pacific Disaster Response Fund: Review of Performance	2015	Asia/Pacific

continued on next page

Table *continued*

Type	Category	Title	Date	Coverage
Event	ENV	Corruption Risks and Anti-Corruption Strategies in Climate Financing: Good Governance Towards Integrity, Transparency, and Accountability in Achieving Objectives in Climate Mitigation and Adaptation—Training Workshop	2015	PHI
Report	ENV	Costing of the National Action Plan of the Philippines	2015	PHI
Working Paper	ENV	Global Increase in Climate-Related Disasters	2015	Asia/PHI
Brief	ENV	Linking Post-Disaster Recovery to Development	2015	PHI
Report	ENV	Proceedings of the Regional Knowledge Forum on Post-Disaster Recovery	2015	Asia/USA/PHI
Presentation	ENV	Status of Climate Finance in the Philippines	2015	PHI
Brief	ENV	Shared Lessons on Post-Disaster Recovery	2015	PHI
Event	ENV	Coastal and Marine Resources Management in the Coral Triangle–Southeast Asia	2014	SEA
Report	ENV	Economics of Fisheries and Aquaculture in the Coral Triangle	2014	Asia/Pacific
Report	ENV	Reconstruction Assistance on Yolanda: Implementation for Results	2014	PHI
Report	ENV	Regional State of the Coral Triangle—Coral Triangle Marine Resources: Their Status, Economies, and Management	2014	Asia/Pacific
Report	ENV	State of the Coral Triangle: Philippines	2014	PHI
Video	ENV	Survivors of Typhoon Haiyan (Yolanda)	2014	PHI
Brochure	ENV	Typhoon Yolanda (Haiyan): Asian Development Bank Assistance	2014	PHI
Brief	ENV	ADB Southeast Asia Support to the Coral Triangle Initiative	2013	SEA
Working Paper	ENV	Climate-Related Disasters in Asia and the Pacific	2013	PHI
Event	ENV	Determining Potential for Carbon Capture and Storage in Southeast Asia (Philippine Workshop)	2013	SEA
Book	ENV	Prospects for Carbon Capture and Storage in the Philippines	2013	PHI
Report	ENV	Reconstruction Assistance on Yolanda: Build Back Better	2013	PHI
Report	ENV	Stakeholder Engagement in Preparing Investment Plans for the Climate Investment Funds: Case Studies from Asia	2013	Asia/PHI
Good Governance and Inclusive Finance				
Presentation	GOV/PSM	Participatory Budgeting in the Philippines	2017	PHI
Brief	GOV/PSM	Taxing Properties and Managing Land: The Many Pathways on a Long Journey in the Philippines	2016	PHI
Event	GOV/PSM	ASEAN Corporate Governance Conference, Manila	2015	SEA/PHI
Report	GOV/PSM	ASEAN Corporate Governance Scorecard: Country Reports and Assessments, 2015	2015	SEA

continued on next page

Table *continued*

Type	Category	Title	Date	Coverage
Brief	GOV/PSM	Building Modern Land Administration Systems	2015	PHI
Brief	GOV/PSM	Fuel-Marking Programs: Helping Governments Raise Revenue, Combat Smuggling, and Improve the Environment	2015	Asia/PHI
Brief	GOV/PSM	Ramping up Results-Based Management in the Philippines	2015	PHI
Event	GOV/PSM	Strengthening Citizen Involvement in Mitigating Governance Risks in Local Government Units in the Philippines	2015	PHI
Report	GOV/PSM	A Comparative Analysis of Tax Administration in Asia and the Pacific	2014	Asia/Pacific
Report	GOV/PSM	ASEAN Corporate Governance Scorecard: Country Reports and Assessments, 2013–2014	2014	SEA
Event	GOV/PSM	Bangsamoro Transition Commission Forum	2014	PHI
Brief	GOV/PSM	How Tobacco Taxes Can Expand Fiscal Space and Benefit the Poor	2014	Asia/PHI
Event	GOV/PSM	Luzon Consultation for the Review of the Local Government Code	2014	PHI
Event	GOV/PSM	Mindanao Consultation for the Review of the Local Government Code	2014	PHI
Strategy	GOV/PSM	Philippine Corporate Governance Blueprint 2015: Building a Stronger Corporate Governance Framework	2015	PHI
Event	GOV/PSM	Philippines Development Forum on Bangsamoro	2014	PHI
Event	GOV/PSM	Reconstructing Accountability After Major Disasters: Closing the Space on Fraud, Corruption, Neglect, and Incompetence in Disaster Relief Programs	2014	PHI
Manual/Guide	GOV/PSM	Results-Based Management Framework in the Philippines	2014	PHI
Event	GOV/PSM	Visayas Consultation for the Review of the Local Government Code	2014	PHI
Report	GOV/PSM	ASEAN Corporate Governance Scorecard: Country Reports and Assessments, 2012–2013	2013	SEA
Book	GOV/PSM	Asian Development Outlook 2013 Update: Governance and Public Service Delivery	2013	Asia/Pacific
Capacity Development	GOV/PSM	Capacity Development of Financial Regulators	2013	PHI
Working Paper	GOV/PSM	Financial Crisis as a Catalyst for Legal Reforms: The Case of Asia	2013	Asia/PHI
Report	GOV/PSM	Forum on Building Resilience to Fragility in Asia and the Pacific: Proceedings	2013	Asia/Pacific
Book	GOV/PSM	Managing Reforms for Development: Political Economy of Reforms and Policy-Based Lending Case Studies	2013	Asia/PHI
Event	GOV/PSM	Presentation by the Judiciary Development Planning Office to the Supreme Court Justices en Banc	2013	PHI
Event	GOV/PSM	The Role of Civil Society Organizations in ADB's Anticorruption and Transparency Work	2013	PHI

continued on next page

Table *continued*

Type	Category	Title	Date	Coverage
Report	GOV/PSM	Tobacco Taxes: A Win–Win Measure for Fiscal Space and Health	2013	Asia/PHI
Brief	GOV/PSM	Environmental Governance and the Courts in Asia: An Asian Judges Network on the Environment	2012	SEA/PHI
Event	GOV/PSM	Good Practices in Land Administration	2012	PHI
Report	GOV/PSM	Philippines Country Procurement Assessment Report, 2012	2012	PHI
Event	GOV/PSM	Results-Based Planning and Budgeting and Evaluation	2012	Asia/Pacific
Report	GOV/PSM	The Philippine Government Electronic Procurement System—Organizational Study	2012	PHI
Report	FIN	ASEAN+3 Bond Market Guide 2017: Philippines	2017	PHI
Report	FIN	Assessment of Microinsurance as Emerging Microfinance Service for the Poor—The Case of the Philippines	2013	PHI
Book	FIN	Financial Inclusion, Regulation, and Education: Asian Perspectives	2017	Asia/PHI
Working Paper	FIN	Credit Surety Fund: A Credit Innovation for Micro, Small, and Medium-Sized Enterprises in the Philippines	2016	PHI
Report	FIN	Disaster-Resilient Microfinance: Learning from Communities Affected by Typhoon Haiyan	2016	PHI
Working Paper	FIN	Assessing Mandated Credit Programs: Case Study of the Magna Carta in the Philippines	2015	PHI
Brief	FIN	PPPs in Information and Communication Technology for Education	2015	Asia/PHI
Working Paper	FIN	Why Do SMEs Not Borrow More from Banks? Evidence from the People's Republic of China and Southeast Asia	2015	Asia/PHI
Capacity Development	FIN	Capacity Building for PPP Center Knowledge Management System	2014	PHI
Working Paper	FIN	Equity Home Bias, Financial Integration, and Regulatory Reforms: Implications for Emerging Asia	2014	Asia/PHI
Report	FIN	Establishing the Typhoon Yolanda Multi-Donor Trust Fund	2014	PHI
Book	FIN	Financial Inclusion in Asia: Country Surveys	2014	Asia/PHI
Event	FIN	National Seminar on Microinsurance	2014	PHI
Report	FIN	PPPs @ PH Investment Opportunities	2014	PHI
Event	FIN	Status of PPP Program in the Philippines	2014	PHI
Report	FIN	Strengthening PPPs in the Philippines: Final Report	2014	PHI
Capacity Development	FIN	Capacity Development of Government Lawyers on PPP	2013	PHI
Working Paper	FIN	Corporate Investments in Asian Emerging Markets: Financial Conditions, Financial Development, and Financial Constraints	2013	SEA

continued on next page

Table *continued*

Type	Category	Title	Date	Coverage
Brief	FIN	Decentralized Loan Management Improves Infrastructure for Rural Productivity	2013	PHI
Manual/Guide	FIN	Guidebook on Public–Private Partnership in Hospital Management	2013	PHI
Manual/Guide	FIN	Guidebook on Public–Private Partnership in Pharmacy	2013	PHI
Report	FIN	Public–Private Partnership in Health: Consultant's Final Report	2013	PHI
Working Paper	FIN	The Threat of Financial Contagion to Emerging Asia's Local Bond Markets: Spillovers from Global Crises	2013	Asia/PHI
Capacity Development	FIN	Training of Trainers for the PPP Center	2013	PHI
Working Paper	FIN	A Welfare Evaluation of Fast Asian Monetary Policy Regimes under Foreign Output Shock	2012	Asia/PHI
Working Paper	FIN	Assessing the Resilience of ASEAN Banking Systems: The Case of the Philippines	2012	PHI
Sector Assessment	FIN	Country Public–Private Partnership Assessment	2012	PHI
Report	FIN	Five Applications in PPP in Health	2012	PHI
Gender Equity				
Brief	GEN	ADB Experiences: Legislating Gender Equality	2014	Asia/PHI
Brief	GEN	Gender Equity and Opportunities in Irrigation	2014	PHI
Report	GEN	Gender Equality and the Labor Market: Cambodia, Kazakhstan, and the Philippines	2013	PHI
Report	GEN	Gender Equality in the Labor Market in the Philippines	2013	PHI
Book	GEN	Impact of Global Crisis on Migrant Workers and Families: Gender Perspective	2013	PHI
Report	GEN	Promoting Gender Equality in Land Access and Land Tenure Security in the Philippines	2013	PHI
Event	GEN	Promoting Gender Equality in the Labor Market for More Inclusive Growth: National Workshop, Philippines	2012	PHI
Education, Skills Development, and Youth Employment				
Brief	EDEM	Reducing Youth Not in Employment, Education, or Training through JobStart Philippines	2018	PHI
Brief	EDEM	Philippines: Senior High School Support Program—Project Brief	2016	PHI
Brochure	EDEM	JobStart Brochure	2015	PHI
Brief	EDEM	JobStart: Impacts and Insights (No. 1)	2015	PHI
Brief	EDEM	Teach for the Philippines, Teach for Development	2015	PHI
Report	EDEM	Transitions to K-12 Education Systems: Experiences from Five Case Countries	2015	Asia/PHI
Event	EDEM	Learning from International Experience: Innovative Public–Private Partnerships in the Education Sector	2014	PHI

continued on next page

Table *continued*

Type	Category	Title	Date	Coverage
Report	EDEM	Computer Access Mentorship Program—A Public–Private Partnership for Enhancing Education Quality: Consultant's Report	2013	PHI
Working Paper	EDEM	Enterprises in the Philippines: Dynamism and Constraints to Employment Growth	2013	PHI
Book	EDEM	Skills Development for Inclusive and Sustainable Growth	2013	Asia/Pacific
Working Paper	EDEM	The Role of International Trade in Employment Growth in Micro- and Small Enterprises: Evidence from Developing Asia	2013	Asia/PHI
Capacity Development	EDEM	Training Modules and Materials for Online Strengthening of Teacher Skills in Reading	2013	PHI
Book	EDEM	Shadow Education: Private Supplementary Tutoring and Its Implications for Policy Makers in Asia	2012	Asia/Pacific
Social Protection, Community-Driven Development, and Labor Market Reform				
Working Paper	SOC	Income and Consumption Inequality in the Philippines: A Stochastic Dominance Analysis of Household Unit Records	2017	PHI
Report	SOC	Enhancing Community-Driven Development through Convergence: A Case Study of Household- and Community-Based Initiatives in Philippine Villages	2016	PHI
Event and Video	SOC	Insight Thursday: Gina Lopez, The BayaniJuan Multi-Sectoral Partnership through ADB-JFPR Assistance	2015	PHI
Brief	SOC	The Social Protection Support Project in the Philippines	2015	PHI
Report	SOC	Results-Based Monitoring and Evaluation System for the Pilot Implementation of CCT for Indigenous Peoples: Consultant's Report	2014	PHI
Report	SOC	Towards Formulating the Capacity Development Framework for Pantawid Pamilya: Consultant's Report	2014	PHI
Report	SOC	Labor Migration, Skills, and Student Mobility in Asia	2014	Asia/Pacific
Event	SOC	Labor Policy Workshop (TA 8335-PHI)	2014	PHI
Working Paper	SOC	Measuring Social Protection Expenditures in Southeast Asia: Estimates Using the Social Protection Index	2014	SEA
Policy Brief	SOC	Social Discount Rate for the Philippines	2014	PHI
Brief	SOC	After Five Years of Pantawid, What Next? A Policy Brief for the Department of Social Welfare and Development	2013	
Capacity Development	SOC	Capacity Development for Social Protection	2013	PHI
Report	SOC	Strengthened Gender Impacts of Social Protection: Consultant's Report	2013	PHI
Working Paper	SOC	Cost Recoverable Tariffs to Increase Access to Basic Services among the Poor Households	2013	PHI

continued on next page

Table *continued*

Type	Category	Title	Date	Coverage
Event	SOC	Does East Asia Have a Working Financial Safety Net?	2013	Asia/PHI
Working Paper	SOC	Globalization, Labor Market Regulation, and Firm Behavior	2013	Asia/PHI
Report	SOC	Improving Local Service Delivery through Community-Driven Development Approach	2013	PHI
Report	SOC	Inclusive Business Study in Philippines	2013	PHI
Working Paper	SOC	Safety Nets and Food Programs in Asia: A Comparative Perspective	2013	PHI
Report	SOC	The Inclusive Business Market in the Philippines	2013	PHI
Report	SOC	Rapid Appraisal Assessment Report on Early Childhood Care and Development and the Pantawid Pamilyang Pilipino Program: Consultant's Report	2012	PHI
Book	SOC	Global Crisis, Remittances, and Poverty in Asia	2012	Asia/PHI
Working Paper	SOC	Inequality of Human Opportunities in Developing Asia	2012	Asia/PHI
Book	SOC	Pension Systems and Old-Age Income Support in East and Southeast Asia: Overview and Reform Direction	2012	Asia/PHI
Book	SOC	Pension Systems in East and Southeast Asia: Promoting Fairness and Sustainability	2012	Asia/PHI
Working Paper	SOC	Reducing Disparities and Enhancing Sustainability in Asian Pension Systems	2012	Asia/PHI
Report	SOC	The KALAHI-CIDSS Project in the Philippines—Sharing Knowledge on Community-Driven Development	2012	PHI
Regional Cooperation and Integration				
Report	RCI	BIMP-EAGA's Economic Corridors: Business Perceptions about the Investment Climate	2017	SEA/PHI
Report	RCI	BIMP-EAGA Investment Opportunities in Corridor Value Chains	2017	SEA/PHI
Strategy	RCI	BIMP-EAGA Vision 2025	2017	SEA/PHI
Report	RCI	Facilitating Foreign Exchange Risk Management for Bond Investments in ASEAN+3	2015	SEA/PHI
Working Paper	RCI	Local Currency Bonds and Infrastructure Finance in ASEAN+3	2015	Asia/PHI
Working Paper	RCI	Realizing an ASEAN Economic Community: Progress and Remaining Challenges	2015	SEA
Event	RCI	2014 BIMP-EAGA Strategic Planning Meeting and Senior Officials Retreat	2014	Asia/PHI
Event	RCI	2nd BIMP-EAGA Trade and Investment Facilitation Cluster Meeting	2014	Asia/PHI
Event	RCI	4th BIMP-EAGA Workshop on Planning and Conduct of Port Security Drills and Exercises	2014	Asia/PHI

continued on next page

Table *continued*

Type	Category	Title	Date	Coverage
Book	RCI	ASEAN 2030: Towards a Borderless Economic Community	2014	SEA
Working Paper	RCI	ASEAN Commercial Policy: A Rare Case of Outward-Looking Regional Integration	2014	Asia/PHI
Event	RCI	ASEAN Financial Inclusion Conference, Yangon	2014	Asia/PHI
Brief	RCI	ASEAN Infrastructure Fund Infographic	2014	Asia/PHI
Report	RCI	BIMP-EAGA Climate Change Vulnerability Assessment	2014	SEA
Manual/Guide	RCI	BIMP-EAGA Project Manual	2014	SEA
Report	RCI	BIMP-EAGA at a Glance: A Statistical Information Brief	2016	SEA
Event	RCI	BIMP-EAGA Maritime Connectivity Workshop	2014	Asia/PHI
Manual/Guide	RCI	BIMP-EAGA Simplified Port Facility Security Plan Guideline	2014	SEA
Event	RCI	BIMP-EAGA Western Mindanao Study Stakeholders' Meeting	2014	Asia/PHI
Capacity Development	RCI	Economic Corridor Development for Competitiveness and Inclusive Growth (IMT-GT, BIMP-EAGA, and GMS)	2014	Asia/PHI
Event	RCI	International Negotiations for Subregional Cooperation (IMT-GT, BIMP-EAGA, and GMS)	2014	Asia/PHI
Event	RCI	Quarantine and Human Health Operational Risk Management Workshop	2014	Asia/PHI
Event	RCI	Third ASEAN Chief Justices' Roundtable on Environment: ASEAN's Environmental Challenges and Legal Responses	2014	SEA
Event	RCI	7th INO-MAL-THA- Growth Triangle and 9th BRU-INO-MAL-PHI East ASEAN Growth Area Summit	2013	SEA
Book	RCI	ASEAN+3: Information on Transaction Flows and Settlement Infrastructures	2013	Asia/PHI
Report	RCI	Broadening the Investor Base for Local Currency Bonds in ASEAN+2 Countries	2013	Asia/PHI
Event	RCI	Inaugural ASEAN Chief Justices' Roundtable on Environment: The Proceedings	2013	SEA
Strategy	RCI	Master Plan on ASEAN Connectivity Implementation	2013	SEA
Event	RCI	Promoting Links and Improving Coordination among the GMS, BIMP-EAGA, IMT-GT, and ASEAN	2013	SEA
Book	RCI	Regional and Subregional Program Links	2013	SEA
Working Paper	RCI	Regional Trade Agreements and Enterprises in Southeast Asia	2013	SEA/PHI
Event	RCI	Second ASEAN Chief Justices' Roundtable on Environment: The Proceedings	2013	SEA
Event	RCI	Support for Trade Facilitation in BIMP-EAGA	2013	SEA

continued on next page

Table *continued*

Type	Category	Title	Date	Coverage
Book	RCI	The ASEAN Economic Community: A Work in Progress	2013	SEA
Working Paper	RCI	The ASEAN Economic Community: Progress, Challenges, and Prospects	2013	SEA
Manual/Guide	RCI	ASEAN +3 Bond Market Guide	2012	Asia/PHI
Working Paper	RCI	Going Regional: How to Deepen ASEAN's Financial Markets	2012	SEA
Working Paper	RCI	Narrowing the Development Divide in ASEAN: The Role of Policy	2012	SEA
Working Paper	RCI	Strengthening the Financial System and Mobilizing Savings to Support More Balanced Growth in ASEAN+3	2012	Asia/PHI
Working Paper	RCI	The PRC's Free Trade Agreements with ASEAN, Japan, Republic of Korea: A Comparative Analysis	2012	SEA
Agriculture and Natural Resources				
Working Paper	ANR	Rice Trade and Price Volatility: Implications on ASEAN and Global Food Security	2013	SEA/PHI
Working Paper	ANR	ASEAN and Global Rice Situation and Outlook	2012	SEA/PHI
Working Paper	ANR	Climate Change and Price Volatility: Can We Count on the ASEAN+3 Emergency Rice Reserve?	2012	SEA/PHI
Working Paper	ANR	Commodities Exchange: Options for Addressing Price Risk and Price Volatility in Rice	2012	SEA/PHI
Working Paper	ANR	Enhancing ASEAN's Resiliency to Extreme Rice Price Volatility	2012	SEA/PHI
Working Paper	ANR	Pre-Feasibility Study of an ASEAN Rice Futures Market	2012	SEA/PHI
Other Sectors				
Brief	HEA	Knowledge Database Helps Policy Makers Identify and Assess Toxic Waste Hotspots	2015	Asia/Pacific
Event	HEA	Celebrating International Women's Health Day— Reproductive Health Challenges in the Philippines	2014	PHI
Working Paper	ICT	The Information Technology and Business Process Outsourcing Industry: Diversity and Challenges in Asia	2013	Asia/PHI
Brief	Multisector	ADB and the Philippines: Fact Sheet	2012–2017 Annually	PHI
Brief	Multisector	Annual Meeting Briefing Notes	2012–2017 Annually	PHI
Report	Multisector	Asian Development Outlook Update: Subregional Assessment and Prospects (Southeast Asia)	2012–2017 Annually	SEA
Working Paper	Multisector	Dynamic Poverty Decomposition Analysis: An Application to the Philippines	2014	PHI
Working Paper	Multisector	Critical Review of East Asia–South America Trade	2013	Asia/PHI

continued on next page

Table *continued*

Type	Category	Title	Date	Coverage
Working Paper	Multisector	Understanding Innovation in Production Networks in East Asia	2013	Asia/PHI
Strategy	Multisector	Philippines Country Knowledge Strategy and Plan	2012	PHI
Report	Multisector	Purchasing Power Parity Update for Selected Economies in Asia and Pacific: A Research Study	2012	Asia/Pacific
Event	Multisector	The Far Hope of Youth—Working Towards a National Vision	2012	PHI
Working Paper	Multisector	Subnational Purchasing Power Parities Integration of International Comparison Program and Consumer Price Index: The Case of the Philippines	2011	PHI

ADB = Asian Development Bank, ASEAN = Association of Southeast Asian Nations, BIMP-EAGA = Brunei Darussalam–Indonesia–Malaysia–Philippines East ASEAN Growth Area, GMS = Greater Mekong Subregion, IMT-GT = Indonesia–Malaysia–Thailand Growth Triangle, PHI = Philippines, SEA = Southeast Asia, USA = United States of America.

Categories: ANR = Agriculture and Natural Resources; EDEM = Education and Employment; EDP = Economic Development and Poverty Reduction; ENE = Energy Infrastructure; ENV = Environment, Climate Change, and Disaster Risk Reduction; FIN = Inclusive Finance; GEN = Gender; GOV/PSM = Good Governance and Public Sector Management; HEA = Health; ICT = Information and Communications Technology; RCI = Regional Cooperation and Integration; SOC = Social Protection; ST = Sustainable Transport; URB = Urban Infrastructure; WAT = Water and Sanitation.

Source: ADB Philippines Country Office.

References

Asian Development Bank (ADB). 2008. *Developing Microinsurance Project*. Manila.

———. 2009a. *Credit for Better Health Care Project*. Manila.

———. 2009b. *Technical Assistance for the Governance and Capacity Development Initiative (Phase 2)*. Manila.

———. 2009c. *Technical Assistance for Regional Cooperation on Knowledge Management, Policy, and Institutional Support to the Coral Triangle Initiative*. Manila.

———. 2010a. *Decentralized Framework for Sustainable Natural Resources and Rural Infrastructure Management*. Manila.

———. 2010b. *Technical Assistance for Promoting an Interlinked ASEAN Capital Market*. Manila.

———. 2010c. *Republic of the Philippines: Computer Access Mentorship Program—A Public–Private Partnership for Enhancing Education Quality*. Manila.

———. 2010d. *Technical Assistance for Promoting Gender Equality in the Labor Market for More Inclusive Growth*. Manila.

———. 2010e. *Social Protection Support Project*. Manila.

———. 2010f. *Support to Achieve the ASEAN Economic Community and Accelerate the Narrowing of Development Gaps by 2015*. Manila.

———. 2010g. *Technical Assistance for Support for Trade Facilitation in the Brunei Darussalam–Indonesia–Malaysia–Philippines East ASEAN Growth Area*. Manila.

———. 2011a. *Country Partnership Strategy Philippines, 2011–2016*. Manila.

———. 2011b. *Philippines: Private Sector Development: Challenges and Possible Ways to Go*. Manila.

———. 2011c. *Strengthening Public–Private Partnerships in the Philippines*. Manila.

———. 2011d. *Technical Assistance for Supporting Water Operators' Partnerships in Asia and the Pacific*. Manila.

———. 2011e. *Technical Assistance to the Philippines for Support to Local Government Revenue Generation and Land Administration Reforms*. Manila.

ADB. 2012a. SERD Knowledge Management Framework. Manila. Unpublished.

———. 2012b. *Country Operations Business Plan: Philippines, 2013–2015. Country Knowledge Strategy and Plan, 2012–2015*. Manila.

———. 2012c. *Taking the Right Road to Inclusive Growth: Industrial Upgrading and Diversification in the Philippines*. Manila.

———. 2012d. *The Service Sector in Asia: Is it an Engine of Growth?* Manila.

———. 2012e. *Technical Assistance to the Philippines for the Davao Sustainable Urban Transport Project*. Manila.

———. 2012f. *Promoting Innovations in Wastewater Management in Asia and the Pacific*. Manila.

———. 2012g. *Integrated Natural Resources and Environmental Management Project*. Manila.

———. 2012h. *Strengthening Knowledge-Based Economic and Social Development*. Manila.

———. 2012i. *Technical Assistance to the Philippines for Enhancing Social Protection through Community-Driven Development Approach*. Manila.

———. 2012j. *Knowledge First: Progressing Knowledge Management in the Southeast Asia Department, 2010–2011*. Manila.

———. 2013a. *Leveraging Service Sector Growth in the Philippines*. Manila.

———. 2013b. *The Information Technology and Business Process Outsourcing Industry: Diversity and Challenges in Asia*. Manila.

———. 2013c. *Guidebook on Public–Private Partnership in Hospital Management*. Manila.

———. 2013d. *Guidebook on Public–Private Partnership in Pharmacy*. Manila.

———. 2013e. *Davao Sustainable Urban Transport Comprehensive Public Transport Strategy. Davao Sustainable Urban Transport: Final Report*. Manila.

———. 2013f. *Davao Sustainable Urban Transport: Final Report*. Manila.

———. 2013g. Philippines: Climate Change Vulnerability Atlas for Priority River Basins. Unpublished.

———. 2013h. Baseline Information and Vulnerability Assessment Report. Unpublished.

———. 2013i. Civil Society Organization Contributions Toward Improving Public Procurement in the Philippines: Strengthening Constructive Engagement Processes. Unpublished.

———. 2013j. *Assessment of Microinsurance as Emerging Microfinance Service for the Poor: The Case of the Philippines*. Manila.

———. 2013k. *Philippines: Employment Facilitation for Inclusive Growth*. Manila.

——. 2013l. *Impact of the Global Crisis on Asian Migrant Workers and Their Families: A Survey-Based Analysis with a Gender Perspective.* Manila.

——. 2013m. *Support to Community-Based Disaster Risk Management in Southeast Asia.* Manila.

——. 2013n. *Sector Assessment (Summary): Community-Driven Development.* Manila.

——. 2013o. *Report and Recommendation of the President to the Board of Directors: Proposed Loan to the Republic of the Philippines for KALAHI–CIDSS National Community-Driven Development Project.* Manila.

——. 2013p. *Knowledge Management Directions and Action Plan (2013–2015): Supporting "Finance ++" at the Asian Development Bank.* Manila.

——. 2014a. *Midterm Review of Strategy 2020: Meeting the Challenges of a Transforming Asia and Pacific.* Manila.

——. 2014b. *Learning from International Experience: Innovative Public–Private Partnerships in the Education Sector (Philippines).* 26–27 November. http://www.adb.org/news/events/learning-international-experience-innovative-public-private-partnerships-education.

——. 2014c. *From Toilets to Rivers: Experiences, Opportunities, and Innovative Solutions.* Manila.

——. 2014d. Knowledge Products: Decentralized Framework for Sustainable Natural Resources and Rural Infrastructure Management, Philippines. Unpublished.

——. 2014e. Good Governance and Anticorruption in Public Education. June 17. http://www.adb.org/site/integrity/activities.

——. 2014f. *ASEAN Corporate Governance Scorecard: Country Reports and Assessments, 2013–2014.* Manila.

——. 2014g. *Typhoon Yolanda (Haiyan).* Asian Development Bank Assistance. Manila.

——. 2015a. *Strengthening Institutions for Investments in Mindanao.* Manila.

——. 2015b. Experiences from Post-Typhoon Yolanda Recovery Planning and Implementation. Unpublished.

——. 2015c. *Proceedings of the Regional Knowledge Forum on Post-Disaster Recovery.* 20–21 October. Manila.

——. 2015d. Working Paper on Local Good Governance in the Philippines. Unpublished.

——. 2015e. *Assessing Mandated Credit Programs: Case Study of the Magna Carta in the Philippines.* Manila.

——. 2015f. *Realizing an ASEAN Economic Community: Progress and Remaining Challenges.* Manila.

——. 2015g. Status of Climate Finance in the Philippines. Paper presented at the Workshop on Corruption Risks and Anticorruption Strategies in Climate Finance held in Manila, Philippines on 25–27 May.

——. 2017. *Scaling Up Infrastructure Investment in the Philippines: Role of Public–Private Partnership and Issues.* Manila.

——. 2018a. *Strategy 2030: Achieving a Prosperous, Inclusive, Resilient, and Sustainable Asia and the Pacific.* Manila.

———. 2018b. *Country Partnership Strategy: Philippines, 2018–2023—High and Inclusive Growth.* Manila.

———. 2018c. *Philippines: Country Operations Business Plan (2019–2021).* Manila.

ADB, Government of Australia, Coral Triangle Initiative (CTI), and Global Environment Facility (GEF). 2014. *Economics of Fisheries and Aquaculture in the Coral Triangle.* Manila.

ADB, CTI, and GEF. 2014a. *Regional State of the Coral Triangle—Coral Triangle Marine Resources: Their Status, Economies, and Management.* Manila.

———. 2014b. *State of the Coral Triangle: Philippines.* Manila.

ADB and Manila Water Company, Inc. 2014. *Tap Secrets: The Manila Water Story.* Manila.

Asian Development Bank Institute (ADBI). 2017. *The Impact of Improved Transport Connectivity on Income, Education, and Health: The Case of the Roll-On/Roll-Off System in the Philippines.* Tokyo.

Brunei Darussalam–Indonesia–Malaysia–Philippines East ASEAN Growth Area (BIMP-EAGA). 2014. *Common Guidebook Simplified Port Facility Security Plan for Secondary Port Facilities.* Manila.

Coral Triangle Initiative (CTI). 2009. *Coral Triangle Initiative: Regional Plan of Action.* Jakarta.

———. 2015. *Costing of the National Plan of Action (NPOA) of the Philippines.* Manila.

Das, S. B. et al., eds. 2013. *The Asian Economic Community: A Work in Progress.* Singapore: Institute of Southeast Asian Studies.

National Economic and Development Authority (NEDA). 2013. *Reconstruction Assistance on Yolanda: Build Back Better.* Manila.

———. 2014. *Reconstruction Assistance on Yolanda: Implementation for Results.* Manila.

———. 2017. *AmBisyon Natin 2040.* http://2040.neda.gov.ph/.

Philippine Institute for Development Studies (PIDS). 2013. *After Five Years of Pantawid, What Next?* Manila.

Public-Private Partnership Center. 2012. *A PPP Manual for Local Government Units.* Vols. 1–3. Manila.

Securities and Exchange Commission (SEC). 2015. *Philippine Corporate Governance Blueprint 2015: Building a Stronger Corporate Governance Framework.* Manila.

www.ingramcontent.com/pod-product-compliance
Lightning Source LLC
Chambersburg PA
CBHW050056220326
41599CB00045B/7436